THE FEAR OF THE LORD IS WISDOM

KRISTIAN PEREZ

Unless otherwise indicated, all Scripture quotations are taken from the King James Version of the Bible.

Scripture quotations marked NKJV are taken from the New King James Version, copyright © 1979, 1980, 1982, Thomas Nelson, Inc. Publishers. Used by permission. All rights reserved.

Scripture quotations marked NIV are taken from the Holy Bible, New International Version®. NIV®. Copyright © 1973, 1978, 1984 by International Bible Society. Used by permission of Zondervan Publishing House. All rights reserved.

The author has emphasized some words in Scripture quotations in italicized type.

The Fear of the Lord is Wisdom
ISBN: 0-88144-385-9
Copyright © 2009 by Kristian Perez

Published by
Thorncrown Publishing
A Division of Yorkshire Publishing Group
9731 East 54th Street
Tulsa, Oklahoma 74146
www.yorkshirepublishing.com

Printed in the United States of America. All rights reserved under International Copyright Law. Contents and/or cover may not be reproduced in whole or in part in any form without the express written consent of the Publisher.

CONTENTS

Introduction 9
1 Seeking Wisdom 13
2 Wisdom in Words 17
3 Trading Weakness for Strength 24
4 The Rewards of Wisdom 27
5 Be Angry and Sin Not 30
6 Freedom 32
7 Humility 34
8 Wisdom in Relationships 37
9 Christ vs. Religion 40
10 Time Management 42
11 Obedience 44
12 Understanding 47
13 Solitude 53
14 Change 55
15 Evaluate 59
16 Wisdom to Serve 65
17 Impact 69
18 Compassion 73
19 Think 75
20 Distractions 79
21 Thoughts 83

22	The Gift	87
23	Great Power	91
24	Your Armor	97
25	Reactions	102
26	ACT	104
27	Questions	107
28	Committed	111
29	Masks	115
30	Yourself	118
31	Endorsement	120
32	Work	122
33	People	124
34	Do Good	127

Conclusion	135
Acknowledgement	137
Notes	139

INTRODUCTION

I share my story only to show God's mercy and that His hand was on me, even when I didn't care about Him at all. He was faithful to me and put a heart in me to understand His wisdom. He will be faithful to you as well.

I was born Catholic and was raised by a very decent family—my grandparents. I never knew my father, and my mother was in and out most of my life.

I always wanted to be a police officer. I thought it would be the greatest *job* and career in the world. I was in the security field and worked as security officer, then as a security instructor and manager for many years.

In 2004, I was hired by a police department and entered the academy. I suffered on all levels—physically, spiritually, and emotionally. I took it personally and that made it worse. I graduated from the academy but then injured myself, tearing my ACL (anterior ligament.) It was a long road to recovery and I struggled during that time. But God searched for me and kept me. God is greater than our problems.

I finally made it on my own through that difficult time and then *it* happened. On I went to roll call as I did every day. I had previously been assigned to a hospital detail—watching a prisoner, but on that day, November 5, 2006, there was no hospital detail and instead, I was on patrol.

It was a Sunday morning and my first call was a domestic dispute. I arrived at the scene with my partner in a separate car. We

THE FEAR OF THE LORD IS WISDOM

picked up the victim and took him to the location where he said he had his possessions. When I arrived I saw a nearly naked man covered in blood, yelling and screaming in the alley. My partner got lost on the way and I was dealing with this insane and emotionally traumatized person alone. I was forced to use my Taser on him several times and tried to take him into custody. I do not know how, but he threw a door at me. I ran after him and used my Taser on him again and again but it had no effect at all, as if it hadn't even happened. I commanded him to calm down and to comply. Nothing was working. He said he had AIDS and used some sort of witchcraft to curse me. He was throwing all kinds of things at me.

Well, here is where my story starts.

I was in shock at this point and *scared*. I said to myself, *My God! I could be fired, or worse, have criminal charges. That's it; my life is over—my career, my dreams done.* I was taken to the hospital with the rest of the officers to get checked for diseases because while I was trying to subdue him, I was exposed to his blood. That's all I thought about. *How can I touch, kiss, or even live with my wife? It's over.* I spoke with the attorney who arrived on the scene of the shooting, still in shock and scared. I went home that day at 8:00 p.m.—a day that started at 7:00 a.m. and forever changed me.

The story was all over the news—everywhere, everyone *knew*.

That night the calls were coming in. Internal Affairs was on the scene. I called an officer that was on the scene while I was in another

INTRODUCTION

officer's patrol car, thinking I could talk to him about what just happened. I said to him, "Please talk to me, anything. I am dying right here, right now." He said, "Don't call me." I couldn't even talk to my fellow officer. I thought I was going to die.

There are moments in life that change everything. Your reaction will have either a positive or a negative lasting effect. Think on this: there are defining moments in people's lives where they need a friend. Your support for that person at that particular moment can mean everything to them.

How we react or fail to react changes everything. I thought of a million bad, horrible outcomes—divorce, in jail, without a home. I mean I was dying inside. I felt like saying or screaming, "Does anyone care? I am right here. I need anyone, right now."

I was cleared two years later. Thank you God, amen.

Even though that incident was very bad, God has used it for good in my life. I was forever changed and it was not long until I gave my life to the Lord. My quest has been to study the Scriptures and find the wisdom of God for every situation. If I had known God's wisdom that terrible night, I think the outcome would have been very different. God's wisdom comes alive in us as we study His words—so we can learn and grow wise, so that we can prosper and be a blessing to others. Then we will have His wisdom and His peace when we are in difficult situations. It's this insight that I want to share with you in the pages to follow.

Wisdom Reflections

1

SEEKING WISDOM

[Wisdom] *is* a tree of life to them that lay hold upon her:
and happy *is every one* that retaineth her.

—PROVERBS 3:18

After the night of November 5, 2006, I began looking for answers for the weaknesses I found in my own life. I found and fell in love with the Bible—primarily Proverbs, which has true words of wisdom. When I was a youth I had even studied theology. God was there, but those desires faded quickly. I took a few classes but I was empty then and other things distracted me.

Even before I knew how to drive, God was there. I took my uncle's car and drove it and almost crashed it. I did hit a small trash can but there was not even a scratch on the car. God was there. They looked and couldn't believe it—no damage to the vehicle. My uncle was getting married that day—God was looking out for me and for him.

THE FEAR OF THE LORD IS WISDOM

There is a bumper sticker that says, "God is my co-pilot." It makes me think, *Thank You, God, because I know you have been busy being my pilot.*

Before I found God, I was seeking wisdom. I guess He just put that in me, but I was looking in all the wrong places. I collected animal totems, mainly foxes and owls because they are considered by certain spiritualists to be wise. I had pictures, paintings, and sculptures of animals. I asked a friend who was an artist to draw a symbol of wisdom for me. To my surprise, he gave me a picture of Christ with a child. Now I recognize that incident was Christ talking to me. God was there.

Even before I accepted Christ, Christ sought me. "But God demonstrates His own love toward us, in that while we were still sinners, Christ died for us" (Romans 5:8 NKJV). Jesus loves us. He came to save that which was lost—me and you, all of us. Jesus Christ searches for you every day. Don't ever doubt it.

The book of Proverbs says, "The fear of the Lord is the beginning of wisdom, and knowledge of the Holy One is understanding" (9:10 NIV). The Lord was seeking me and when I finally connected with Him, I found the wisdom I was looking for.

Conversations with God

ME: Why God, why me? Why did I go to work that day? Why did I have to get that call? Where are You in all this? Why do I have to go through this trial, why did I have to make this kind of mistake? WHERE ARE YOU?

GOD: Right here with you. I am not hiding, I am right here.

ME: Why am I going through this?

GOD: Going through what?

ME: Are you kidding me? I mean, is this a joke? My life is over. I will be fired or worse, criminally charged. What do you know about my pain?

GOD: Let's look at the situation together. Let's see, you still have your job. They gave you a city gun. You have the attorney who arrived on the scene. You have your access card. You have your health, your mind, and guess who else you have right now, right here?

ME: I don't know. Who?

GOD: Me! I Am your gift. I Am your reward. I Am your salvation.

ME: Okay, I see. So you wanted me to learn to trust You and know that You are really there.

GOD: Who else can you lean on or really *trust?*

ME: Nobody but You, but why did I have to go through this? Why didn't You get my attention another way? Why this way? Why did You allow this to happen to me?

GOD: What did I allow?

ME: You allowed me the opportunity to know You, see You, understand You're in control, and that You are my shield, my sword, my salvation.

THE FEAR OF THE LORD IS WISDOM

GOD: Very good, you are learning. It's about time. Just kidding.

ME: I did not know You had sense of humor.

GOD: Really, look around you and see and listen. There is joy and laughter all around. Just open your heart, your mind, your soul to me. For with me, the impossible is possible. Nothing is too good, nothing is impossible; nothing is unimaginable for me to do for You. And nothing is too good to last.

ME: Thank You for loving me.

GOD: I Am love. I cannot change what I Am for I do not change ever. I Am that I Am, always and forever.

ME: Why do I and others suffer so much and watch others suffer so much?

GOD: By one man sin entered the world, but because of My love for you, I paid the price Myself.

I died in your place. My body, my mind, my soul hung on that cross. You were bought by Me. I died so you could live and I suffered so you could live. You and the world sinned, yet I came to save that which was lost. I know all about suffering, more than anyone ever could.

Wisdom Reflections

2

WISDOM IN WORDS

[Wisdom] *is* a tree of life to them that lay hold upon her:
and happy *is every one* that retaineth her.

—PROVERBS 3:18

Your words and your actions have power. They affect your life here and in the hereafter. Words can wound hearts and minds but they can also bring life and hope. Be careful what you say. Wise is the man who is silent and even wiser is the person who measures their words.

Instead of saying damaging words to others out of frustration, talk with Christ, your mediator between you and God. Not only does He listen, but He does not talk to anyone about your personal relationship with Him or your sins. Confess your sins, and he will forgive you (1 John 1:9).

When I was about twelve or thirteen, I climbed a tree and could not get down. The firemen had to come with a ladder to rescue me. My grandmother asked how I got up there and why was I up there. I

THE FEAR OF THE LORD IS WISDOM

told her I didn't know but I was talking with God. If only I had continued to do so.

God is trying to get our attention all the time if you will just look and listen. People ask, "Where is God?" He is right here, right now. He was with me on November 5, 2006. God was working behind the scenes for me in His way, not mine. I may have felt like there was no one there, but even when people let you down, God is always there.

When you are upset, give it to God. Say, "God, take this from me. Give me wisdom to replace my anger. God, please give me understanding to replace my weakness." I can think of many times when I begged God for answers, but I did not admit I had sinned. First, admit your sins and ask for forgiveness, and then God will help you.

When you have God's wisdom it's easier to think about other people and their feelings and where they are in their life *right now*. Things can change quickly for people and you have no idea what a person is going through or has gone through in life. Ask God for His wisdom when dealing with others. When someone tells you something, it may mean nothing to you, but the whole world to them. Just like when I called my fellow officer on the night of November 5, 2006, I was hurting and he was not there for me. I want to be there for others when they need me. Think on that and take the time to really hear and listen to the people around you.

WISDOM IN WORDS

Conversations with God

ME: Why, Father, have You taken Your gifts from me?

GOD: Why did you misuse them after all of the warnings?

ME: Please forgive and return to me Your gifts.

GOD: Stop sinning and I will.

ME: Please, please return the gifts to me.

GOD: If I return to you the gifts, what will you do with them?

ME: I will use them to spread Your Word and the good news of salvation through Christ our Lord and Savior and help others come to Christ and also not use them for personal gain. I will help heal and not destroy.

GOD: I will give you back portions of your gifts to see if you are faithful to your words.

ME: God, why can't I have them all back?

GOD: Because you will become proud again, and to save you, I must keep you humble.

ME: For a wise man is humble before God.

GOD: Looks like you already have wisdom. (I made you humble so you would be wise.)

ME: So by gaining humility and losing pride, one becomes wise.

THE FEAR OF THE LORD IS WISDOM

GOD: Humility is the key to all. Think on this: I love all my children. Come humbly before me, and I will grant your heart's desire.

ME: Thank You, Father, through our Lord Jesus Christ and Holy Spirit, for the gifts of the spirit, I pray in Jesus' name. Holy Spirit, grant me wisdom, understanding, and counsel. In Jesus' name, may the spirit of the Holy One dwell in me forever, amen.

GOD: What hurts more than any weapon and is not considered a weapon by men and women?

ME: Don't know.

GOD: Your words! Your tongue can destroy as much or more than any weapon.

ME: How? They are just words.

GOD: How many lives, marriages, and families are destroyed because of words of hatred or anger?

ME: I have said a lot of things I regret.

GOD: Do you think that you have not caused much pain in other people lives?

ME: Yes, I do.

GOD: Does it take longer to create or to destroy?

ME: A lot longer to create than to destroy. It takes a lot longer to heal too.

GOD: Think about the things you have said and done that hurt others. Think about those whom you do not like and why you don't

WISDOM IN WORDS

like them. It's their words and deeds; it's not them. Your words are not only heard but absorbed.

ME: Yes, I still can think of hurtful things that hurt me; and You are right, they were just words.

GOD: Only words of *life* and *death* are in the tongue. What we say and don't say have both incredible and lasting results.

Wisdom from the Scriptures

Read Proverbs Chapters 1-6 and reflect on words of *life*. Just the first few verses show the results you receive by studying these Scriptures.

> The proverbs of Solomon the son of David, king of Israel; To know wisdom and instruction; to perceive the words of understanding; To receive the instruction of wisdom, justice, and judgment, and equity; To give subtlety to the simple, to the young man knowledge and discretion. A wise *man* will hear, and will increase learning; and a man of understanding shall attain unto wise counsels: To understand a proverb, and the interpretation; the words of the wise, and their dark sayings.
>
> *The fear of the LORD is the beginning of knowledge: but fools despise wisdom and instruction. My son, hear the instruction of thy father, and forsake not the law of thy mother: For they shall be an ornament of grace unto thy head, and chains about thy neck.* (Proverbs 1:1-2)

THE FEAR OF THE LORD IS WISDOM

Conversations with God

ME: Proverbs 1-6, that's a lot to read.

GOD: Read for there is life in My words.

ME: I find it difficult to understand.

GOD: Seek Me. I Am understanding. Seek Me, and it will become plain. Seek Me, and the difficult will be easy. Seek Me, and the impossible becomes not only possible but easy.

ME: Where is wisdom found?

GOD: Read this.

> Surely there is a vein for the silver, and a place for gold *where* they fine *it.* Iron is taken out of the earth, and brass *is* molten *out of* the stone. He setteth an end to darkness, and searcheth out all perfection: the stones of darkness, and the shadow of death. The flood breaketh out from the inhabitant; *even the waters* forgotten of the foot: they are dried up, they are gone away from men. *As for* the earth, out of it cometh bread: and under it is turned up as it were fire. The stones of it *are* the place of sapphires: and it hath dust of gold. *There is* a path which no fowl knoweth, and which the vulture's eye hath not seen: The lion's whelps have not trodden it, nor the fierce lion passed by it. He putteth forth his hand upon the rock; he overturneth the mountains by the roots. He cutteth out rivers among the rocks; and his eye seeth every precious thing. He bindeth the floods from over-

flowing; and *the thing that is* hid bringeth he forth to light. But where shall wisdom be found? And where *is* the place of understanding? Man knoweth not the price thereof; neither is it found in the land of the living.

The depth saith, It *is* not in me: and the sea saith, *It is* not with me. It cannot be gotten for gold; neither shall silver be weighed *for* the price thereof. It cannot be valued with the gold of Ophir, with the precious onyx, or the sapphire. The gold and the crystal cannot equal it: and the exchange of it *shall not be for* jewels of fine gold. No mention shall be made of coral, or of pearls: for the price of wisdom *is* above rubies. The topaz of Ethiopia shall not equal it; neither shall it be valued with pure gold.

Whence then cometh wisdom? And where *is* the place of understanding? Seeing it is hid from the eyes of all living, and kept close from the fowls of the air. Destruction and death say, We have heard the fame thereof with our ears. God understandeth the way thereof, and he knoweth the place thereof. For he looketh to the ends of the earth, *and* seeth under the whole heaven; to make the weight for the winds; and he weigheth the waters by measure. When he made a decree for the rain, and a way for the lightning of the thunder: Then did he see it, and declare it; he prepared it, yea, and searched it out. And unto man he said, *Behold, the fear of the Lord, that is wisdom; and to depart from evil is understanding.* (Job 28: 1-30)

Wisdom Reflections

3

TRADING WEAKNESS FOR STRENGTH

[Wisdom] *is* a tree of life to them that lay hold upon her:
and happy *is every one* that retaineth her.

—PROVERBS 3:18

I recently went to Israel and was baptized in the Jordan River by two men I did not know, yet their nephew sent me a photograph of the event. God spoke to me, "I want you to remember today forever." Israel was the most beautiful place and I felt so close to God, but it was frightening at the same time. The people live in the presence of real terror; there are heavily armed police and military everywhere. I am a police officer, yet I was still nervous.

The churches were the most beautiful I had ever prayed in, but Gethsemane was by far the most important to me because it was where He suffered for us. Christ knows us intimately because He was tempted just as we are. We all have our Gethsemane—our own

TRADING WEAKNESS FOR STRENGTH

struggles with temptation. Go to God, confess, and feel the power of His love, mercy, and grace. Trade your weaknesses for His strength.

I saw the empty tomb of Jesus Christ and knew that He overcame sin, death, and Satan through the power of God. It is the same for you and me. We can overcome our struggles by trusting in God and receiving His strength.

God tells us: "Counsel is mine, and sound wisdom: I am understanding; I have strength" (Prov. 8:14). Stop and think about that truth: God is wisdom and understanding. God can see right through you; He knows your thoughts, fears, hopes, hurts, and sins. He loves you as you are. But He desires for us to change—to grow in our character. God is holy above all, through the sacrifice of Jesus, He sees us as holy. Because He loves us, we have the grace to change.

Our God is the one true God—the only holy God.

Consider what God did with and through Moses. Moses killed a man and ran away from his problems, but God called him and changed him. God used him to help set the nation of Israel free from the slavery of Egypt. God opened the Red Sea and Moses led the people through on dry land.[1] We all have our own Red Sea. Stop trying to part the sea alone and put it in God's mighty and powerful hands to move it out of the way.

When the Lord asked Abraham if there was anything God could not do, Abraham believed and because He believed, God considered him a righteous man. Consider the fact that Abraham was one hundred years old and his wife ninety, yet she bore him a son.[2] God's power can do anything. We all have our own limits, weaknesses, and strengths but only God has strength and no weakness. Seek God in all of your problems. Is there anything the Lord cannot do? No, for with God, all things are possible.[3]

GETHSEMANE

Then cometh Jesus with them unto a place called Gethsemane, and saith unto the disciples, Sit ye here, while I go and pray yonder. And he took with him Peter and the two sons of Zebedee, and began to be sorrowful and very heavy. Then saith he unto them, My soul is exceeding sorrowful, even unto death: tarry ye here, and watch with me. And he went a little further, and fell on his face, and prayed, saying, O my Father, if it be possible, let this cup pass from me: nevertheless not as I will, but as thou *wilt*. And he cometh unto the disciples, and findeth them asleep, and saith unto Peter, What, could ye not watch with me one hour? Watch and pray that ye enter not into temptation: the spirit indeed *is* willing, but the flesh *is* weak. He went away again the second time, and prayed, saying, O my Father, if this cup may not pass away from me, except I drink it, thy will be done. And he came and found them asleep again: for their eyes were heavy. And he left them, and went away again, and prayed the third time, saying the same words. Then cometh he to his disciples, and saith unto them, Sleep on now, and take *your* rest: behold, the hour is at hand, and the Son of man is betrayed into the hands of sinners. Rise, let us be going: behold, he is at hand that doth betray me. (Matthew 26:36-46)

4

THE REWARDS OF WISDOM

[Wisdom] *is* a tree of life to them that lay hold upon her:
and happy *is every one* that retaineth her.

—PROVERBS 3:18

When you begin to follow after God, it really is the beginning of true wisdom. He holds the answers to all of your problems and is willing to work through them, with you no matter how long it takes.

As you seek Christ in all that you do, think, and feel, you will be rewarded in many ways—here on this earth and in your life eternally. Hebrews 6:11 says: "But without faith it is impossible to please him: for he that cometh to God must believe that he is, and that he is a rewarder of them that diligently seek him." When you reach out to others in compassion to be a blessing to them, God rewards you. He tells us to love our neighbors as ourselves and that includes our family.[4] I bring my wife flowers all the time, both at work and at home. Do things to be a blessing to your family. I try to

THE FEAR OF THE LORD IS WISDOM

visit my grandparents every day. We walk the dog and talk and sometimes we share a meal together.

We are selfish by nature and often do not care about others, but God changes us and gives us His nature. I was very selfish and it took a miracle for me to change, but God did it. Men, be willing to change for your wife. Proverbs 18:22 says that a man who finds a wife finds a good thing and receives favor from the Lord. Children are also a blessing from God (Psalm 127: 4-5). Women, please try to support your husband and be understanding. Your reward is not just from your husband, it is from God. And for both men and women, be kind to your in-laws. You are a family—all of you together. Praise God and pray in both good and bad times. Always seek Christ, our Lord and Savior, for His wisdom and help.

Your life is a test. Our faithfulness to God determines our reward. He blesses us so we can be a blessing to others. Take a friend or coworker to lunch; find out about that person. Look for ways to cheer up a friend or family member—take them to the movies or for ice cream or even bring flowers. The Lord will prompt you inside to do things. Be spontaneous; get out of your comfort zone. It has power.

Don't forget to give to the poor and the needy, the lost and the sick. Give not only your money but also your time. And when you give remember the words of Jesus:

> "Be careful not to do your 'acts of righteousness' before men, to be seen by them. If you do, you will have no reward from your Father in heaven. So when you give to the needy, do not announce it with trumpets, as the hypocrites do in

THE REWARDS OF WISDOM

the synagogues and on the streets, to be honored by men. I tell you the truth, they have received their reward in full. But when you give to the needy, do not let your left hand know what your right hand is doing, so that your giving may be in secret. Then your Father, who sees what is done in secret, will reward you. And when you pray, do not be like the hypocrites, for they love to pray standing in the synagogues and on the street corners to be seen by men. I tell you the truth, they have received their reward in full. But when you pray, go into your room, close the door and pray to your Father, who is unseen. Then your Father, who sees what is done in secret, will reward you." (Matthew 6:1-6 NIV)

Please don't forget that everything you do for God will be rewarded. Those who give time, money, love, and effort will be rewarded. In all, be humble. Give to the poor. You can't take it with you, but you can please God and earn rewards in heaven.

Wisdom Reflections

5

BE ANGRY AND SIN NOT

[Wisdom] *is* a tree of life to them that lay hold upon her:
and happy *is every one* that retaineth her.

—PROVERBS 3:18

I have personally struggled with anger. I have begged God to take it from me. Anger is very, very destructive and never helps—it always hurts. The Bible tells us that if we are angry, don't sin. So the anger itself is not a sin, but not controlling your anger is. When you are struggling with sin, go to God for help and He will work through that problem with you. As a believer, you have received God's nature and your old sin nature is dead, but sometimes you have to remind yourself that you are a new creature. Instead of relying on yourself, trust in God to help you.

Put on your new nature, created to be like God—truly righteous and holy. So stop telling lies. Let us tell our neighbors the truth, for we are all parts of the same body. And

BE ANGRY AND SIN NOT

"don't sin by letting anger control you." Don't let the sun go down while you are still angry, for anger gives a foothold to the devil. (Ephesians 4:24-26 NLT)

Because of bitterness, anger or unforgiveness or perhaps due to a destructive event in their lives, many Christians become angry enough to renounce their faith in God. That is a decision that has eternal consequences. Instead of trusting God to help them, they allow the enemy to get a foothold in their lives. Examine your own life. Is there a person you need to forgive? Are you holding a grudge against God? Let it go. Forgive and receive forgiveness. Your eternal destination is worth far more than those bitter feelings.

6

FREEDOM

[Wisdom] *is* a tree of life to them that lay hold upon her: and happy *is every one* that retaineth her.

—PROVERBS 3:18

For me, the cross where Jesus died is the ultimate example of love for us. But I think an even greater example is Gethsemane. It was there that Jesus made the decision to go through with God's plan for our redemption. Jesus prayed not to die three times. Was He scared? Terrified? He was human and God at the same time. He knew what was going to happen to Him and still He loved us more than Himself. God is love.

The Bible says Jesus was in anguish and his sweat was like drops of blood falling to the ground (Luke 22:44). Think about the agony He went through—the pain, the emotional war in His heart, soul, mind, and physical body. We can't even imagine the pain, the depression, and the sorrow Jesus felt. God loved us so much that he came down and humbled himself to suffer and die on the cross. He paid our price for our mistakes—for our souls, for our freedom.

FREEDOM

Think about the war that went on inside of Him, the pain He must have felt all over His body. It is beyond our level of understanding. Christ had a choice the entire time, but He said, "Not my will, but your will, Father."[5] Jesus was always obedient above all.

What would you or I do? We both know the answer. We would not do it. Only God could have paid our price. What would you have done in Jesus' place? What would you have said at that hour of trial and tribulation? I know my answer. I would have failed us all. I would have not passed the ultimate test. Christ passed the test and was victorious. He paid for sin, death, and our freedom. Jesus who knew no sin died so we could become worthy before God.[6] Jesus became sin for us.

When Jesus was brought before the Roman official Pilate, he asked the Jews if they wanted to release Jesus or the convicted murderer Barabbas. The Chief Priests convinced the Jews to choose Barabbas.[7] Who do you think Barabbas *really* was? That's you and me. God let us off the hook—He let us go. He freed us and set us free. Remember God chose us over Himself. That is love. God is the only example of true love.

Wisdom Reflections

7

HUMILITY

[Wisdom] *is* a tree of life to them that lay hold upon her:
and happy *is every one* that retaineth her.

—PROVERBS 3:18

When I was in Israel, I sometimes went twice a day to pray at the Wailing Wall! One day while I was there someone was offended by my cross. I replied, "Let's discuss it." I really meant, *let's argue!* I thought I had the wisdom of God and would win. But God's gifts are not for some childish game. It is serious—very serious—to play with what God gives you. Use His gifts wisely; ask for wisdom in everything at all times. Respect God's gifts and use them with humility for His glory and the benefit of others.

It's very sad to see a man or woman of God, anointed with His power, fall into sin and lose the use of their gift and anointing. Consider the television evangelists or ministers in your community who have been caught in sin or misusing their gifts. They have lost their great reward with God. God is not to be mocked or toyed with. Do not ask for a special gift or anointing unless you fear God and

HUMILITY

will use it with respect, love, and honor. Be wise and careful with all that God gives you including your money, your job or career, and your earthly and spiritual gifts. Do not forget you can lose that which is given; I know I have. Be humble above all before our God.

Even great men and women of the Bible failed God. I will not judge them because I have failed God many times. When you willfully sin, you separate yourself from God. You have to confess your sin and repent. It's difficult; I know. I struggle every day—try every minute. As Jesus said, let him who is without sin cast the first stone.[8] We all have our own struggles with sin, but we also have a Redeemer. Go to your Gethsemane—your garden, your private place—and confess your sins. Tell Him you want to change. Ask Him to give you wisdom, strength, and power to overcome sin through Christ, our Lord and Savior. Through Him, all things are possible.[9] Even the impossible is possible with God. God can do anything if you will allow Him. Admit your weaknesses and receive His strength. You can't do it on your own. Only He can save you and help you. Through Christ you become a new creature—your nature is changed (2 Corinthians 5:17). God knows you—all of you and He knows how to help you.

Consider that God *is* wisdom, understanding, and counsel. He can see right through you. Do not be afraid. Come to Him humbly. You can approach the King of Kings and Lord of Lords because of the price Jesus paid for you, but you must be humble, sincere, repentant, and willing to receive His help. God resists the proud but gives grace to the humble.[10] You can tell Him anything for He already knows everything. He is understanding. He is wisdom.

THE FEAR OF THE LORD IS WISDOM

Conversations with God

ME: Who demonstrated true humility?

GOD: Look at Philippians, Chapter 2:1-11.

If *there be* therefore any consolation in Christ, if any comfort of love, if any fellowship of the Spirit, if any bowels and mercies, Fulfill ye my joy, that ye be likeminded, having the same love, *being* of one accord, of one mind. *Let* nothing *be done* through strife or vainglory; but in lowliness of mind let each esteem others better than themselves. Look not every man on his own things, but every man also on the things of others.

Let this mind be in you, which was also in Christ Jesus: Who, being in the form of God, thought it not robbery to be equal with God: *But made himself of no reputation, and took upon him the form of a servant, and was made in the likeness of men: And being found in fashion as a man, he humbled himself, and became obedient unto death, even the death of the cross. Wherefore God also hath highly exalted him, and given him a name which is above every name: That at the name of Jesus every knee should bow, of things in heaven, and things in earth, and things under the earth; And that every tongue should confess that Jesus Christ is Lord, to the glory of God the Father.*

Wisdom Reflections

8

WISDOM IN RELATIONSHIPS

[Wisdom] *is* a tree of life to them that lay hold upon her:
and happy *is every one* that retaineth her.

—PROVERBS 3:18

God made us to have relationships with each other. They bring us the most happiness and the most heartache. Remember Jesus said to love our neighbor as we love ourselves?[11] That means both people in a relationship should give as much as possible. When you don't give in any area, the relationship suffers.

Take a minute to think about your relationships. Are you a giver or a taker? Be honest with yourself. If you are married, consider your relationship with your spouse and ask yourself, *what does my spouse think about me?* How do you treat them on a daily basis? I have bought my wife flowers every Valentine's Day for years and many times for no reason at all. Guys, it really makes a difference. Ladies, try to surprise your man with a beautifully home cooked meal or a slice of his favorite cake. The lesson here is: learn to give. Giving always makes the giver and the recipient feel good.

Examine my situation with my grandfather—*what a hero.* I never knew my father yet my grandfather raised me as his own and loved me. Now in his later years, it's hard to see him so dependent on my grandmother. It hurts me to see both of them that way. He helped me so many times in the past; I'd like to be able to help him now. When I was eighteen years old, I did some very stupid things and he got me through all of it. I will never forget what he did for me or his kindness.

CONSIDER WISDOM'S WAY

When you fight with a loved one or friend, before you say, "That's it; it's over," remember all the good that person has done for you. It's important. What has that person gone through with you? Remember that shoulder you cried on and that person who sat down and listened to you for endless hours or was on the phone with you when you needed them—for days, weeks, even years. When you think of them in that way, how does that make you feel? Who gave to you and how have you given to people? Do not hold grudges. They are a sin and they destroy you from the inside out. Consider what that other person is going through in their life right now that maybe you just don't understand. Love them like Jesus would love them. Love covers a multitude of sins.[12]

WISDOM IN RELATIONSHIPS

A good friend and I met because his mother was dying of cancer. We bonded in a very special way; to this day, he says I helped him get through that difficult time. Evidence of good and noble acts has lasting rewards. Sinful deeds, however, have lasting negative effects. Trust me, I know.

Wisdom Reflections

9

CHRIST VS. RELIGION

[Wisdom] *is* a tree of life to them that lay hold upon her: and happy *is every one* that retaineth her.

—PROVERBS 3:18

Who do you consider wise? Did they create the earth, the heavens, the sea, the human race, the animals, the universe? What have they done that is so great?

God has been, is, and will always be. Nothing was before He was and He will exist eternally. Can any wise person or so called "god" claim that? Have they died and come back from the dead? Have they raised anyone from the dead or performed any miracles? Have they ever done anything like the miracles of Jesus Christ? Is there anyone like our God—anyone?

People talk about all those religions. Which god is still alive today? Name one who conquered sin, death, and Satan? Jesus, a sinless man, not only died on the cross, but He came back from the

CHRIST VS. RELIGION

dead. Can any other religion make the claim that their god came back from the dead? I used to be into magic, spirits, and animal totems; not one of them can do anything. They are false gods. It's empty; animals die and do not come back. Only Jesus Christ came back. People ask why I follow Christ. I ask them, "Well, tell me who else came back from the dead? Who else could bear what He bore and be sinless before God?" Who else is there but Christ? I tell you the truth; only by the blood of Jesus Christ can anyone be saved. Only through His work and not ours are we saved. Never forget that.

If you were to make a list of all the good things you have done in your life and then a list of all the bad, which one would be longer? But I tell you the truth, because God loves us and gave Jesus in place for our sins, we are blameless before Him; we can walk up to His throne through Christ. Being bold and yet humble, we are children of God. You can tell the world and Satan, "I belong to God and I am a child of God. God loves me." Someone at work told me his thoughts about hell. I replied, "Not me, maybe you. God has already paid for my entrance to heaven; I belong to Him. I already have the ticket in my hand. I am just waiting to get in." Heaven is Christ's gift to us. "For by grace are ye saved through faith; and that not of yourselves: it is the gift of God: not of works, lest any man should boast" (Ephesians 2:8-9). You cannot earn heaven or God's favor. It's earned only through the holy name of Jesus Christ, our Lord and Savior.

If someone says I am lost because of my faith in Christ, I respond by telling them that Jesus came to save the lost. I'm not trying to avoid God's ways; I steer my life on the path of Christ. Stay on God's path.

Wisdom Reflections

10

TIME MANAGEMENT

> [Wisdom] *is* a tree of life to them that lay hold upon her:
> and happy *is every one* that retaineth her.
>
> —PROVERBS 3:18

Examine the evidence of where your time is spent and consider its worth. Look at your phone bills and the calls you made, the text messages you received and sent. Who are you communicating with, how long did it take, and what did you talk about? Was it time well spent with some kind of eternal value?

Look at the books on your shelves, the magazines you subscribe to, the movies you own or rent. What programs do you watch on TV? Really look around—look in your closet, under the bed, in your car, your office, your screen saver, your paintings on the wall. Take a good hard look; has anything changed within you since you turned to God? Take a look at your photographs and think about who you were with, what you felt, and what you were doing. Was there any eternal value?

TIME MANAGEMENT

What's more important to you, here or forever? Are you seeking Christ in what you do and with what God has given you? Don't spend your time judging others who may not have as good a job as you, or the same lifestyle, or the same quality of living or education. You have no idea what has put them in that position. God has blessed you—be thankful and try to use your time for His glory. You have a destiny in God and so does everyone who will seek Him. Instead of judging others, try to help others. "For whosoever exalteth himself shall be abased; and he that humbleth himself shall be exalted (Luke 14:11). Have compassion for others that are not doing as well as you; show mercy and help them in any way you can. Don't make fun or laugh at anyone who is sick, or disabled, or in an unfortunate situation. Use your time for God's glory. He sees all, hears all, and knows all. Nothing, I mean nothing, is hidden from him. Be kind and compassionate for your reward in heaven will be great. Above all, be humble before God. God loves a humble spirit and man or woman that fears him. The fear or reverence of the Lord will save you. Reverence for God protects you and saves in every way. Try to be faithful to God and obedient even when you don't agree or understand—even when you feel like it is too difficult or pointless. Wisdom will always protect you; its very nature is protection. Wisdom is like a tree whose branches cover you and protect you. Wisdom is life.

Wisdom Reflections

11

OBEDIENCE

[Wisdom] *is* a tree of life to them that lay hold upon her:
and happy *is every one* that retaineth her.

—PROVERBS 3:18

Even when God does not make any sense, obedience will save you and protect you. Jesus referred to Himself as the great shepherd and His disciples as His sheep.[13] Sheep follow after the shepherd and obey him because they trust him. The shepherd cares for them and protects them. It's the same when we follow the laws of God; it always benefits us in every way. Consider the wisdom in the Ten Commandments; they protect us from the problems in life. Love God, don't worship anything but God, don't take His name in vain, keep the Sabbath day holy, honor your father and mother, don't lie, don't steal, don't be envious, don't commit adultery, don't kill innocent people (Exodus 20).

Look at society today—on the news or the Internet, in the newspapers and magazines and around your local community. Much of it is not pretty. Many have forgotten the Ten Commandments or

OBEDIENCE

have never even heard of them. They have nothing to guide them. High school dropouts, college dropouts, life dropouts—I see them every day and it pains me because I know what it's like not to have a dream. You feel lost and as if you are not getting any closer to your greatest desires—having a family, buying that new house, having that baby, taking that vacation, or buying that car you really need. Our society is lost without God. Even those who are prospering, are empty inside without God. All the human wisdom in the world is empty without God.

Obedience is the key to our salvation and our hope in this life. Jesus said if you love me, keep my commandments.[14] "Once saved, always saved" is not a true principle; you can lose your salvation if you choose to walk away from God and to continue to sin without thought of His sacrifice. Accepting Christ does not give you a license to sin. It's not a pass to sin or to be disobedient to God's Word. Some say "It's okay, I am covered." But if you search the Scriptures you'll find those people who are disobedient are eventually brought before the Lord. Even though they supposedly did many wonderful works in His name, He says to them, "I never knew you." [Add Scripture Reference] Please think on the fact you must repent to be saved; you cannot continue in willful sin. That's not to say we don't ever sin, but we are aware of it and we try to avoid it instead of bathing in it as others do. It's not okay to sin. Some people say they have accepted Christ, but then they respond with, "Okay, let's party! Let's have fun. We've got the best insurance in the universe—the blood of Christ." If that is your belief, you are eternally mistaken.

THE FEAR OF THE LORD IS WISDOM

Some say the Ten Commandments do not really exist. Consider the teaching of Jesus—He said He came not to do away with the law but to fulfill the law. [Add Scripture here] They exist, and it's not only wise to follow them, but your salvation depends on it. Your faith is dead without actions that prove out what you have said. [Add Scripture here] You cannot accept Christ and just jump into sin. If you have truly accepted Christ, you are a new creature. Old things have passed away and all things have become new.[15] Examine the movies you watch, the music you listen to, and the people you call your friends. Are they different than before you were saved? Do they bring glory to God? You will truly feel better and closer to God when you fill your life with things that honor Him.

"Let us hear the conclusion of the whole matter: Fear God, and keep his commandments: for this *is* the whole *duty* of man. For God shall bring every work into judgment, with every secret thing, whether *it be* good, or whether *it be* evil" (Ecclesiastes 12:13-14).

Wisdom Reflections

12

UNDERSTANDING

[Wisdom] *is* a tree of life to them that lay hold upon her:
and happy *is every one* that retaineth her.

—PROVERBS 3:18

Wisdom may be easy to define, but what is understanding? Understanding encompasses the whole picture. Being able to understand someone, something, or anything determines how you look at things and process information. It determines your frame of thinking.

Understanding *comes from God,* but for a moment, let's look at it from our limited view. For example, when I asked my wife to marry me I knew she wanted to have a family, but I was not thrilled about having children. I really did not think it was that important even though the thought crossed my mind that it would eventually be a problem. I only looked at it from my point of view. I did not have any understanding of my wife's point of view. There are times when we only care about what is important to us. That is a lack of understanding. There came a day when I had to spend time really listening to my wife and looking into her eyes. Then I understood that,

THE FEAR OF THE LORD IS WISDOM

from her point of view, a child was not negotiable. I knew I had to change to make my marriage successful. But I could not, because I would not. So God helped me out with that. He searched me like He searches us all and He changed me.

God is understanding; there is nothing God does not know, nothing that he cannot fully comprehend. God can pierce right through us to reveal the unknown, the hidden secrets of our hearts. I beg for God to give me more understanding daily. It is one of God's greatest gifts because it's pure in essence and does not judge. Understanding is full of compassion. God knows what we go through and helps us. When Jesus was on the earth He felt tired, hungry, and sad just as we do; He was human and God. Because He was human, He understands our emotions and our physical limitations. The ability to see the big picture is important for our success and only God can fully give us that ability.

When I understood how important it was for my wife to start a family, I began to look at all the consequences of that decision. Our life was going to change and I would have to prepare. Having a child is a very big responsibility. You need to be mature enough to determine if you can handle raising a child. *True understanding* looks at all the consequences of our choices. When you look at who will be affected and how they'll be impacted, it changes everything.

There are so many children in single parent homes because the mothers and fathers did not use wisdom and did not have understanding. To have sex with someone that you are not legally married to is a sin. God understands that it damages all the parties involved and He gave His law so that we would be free from that pain. Look

UNDERSTANDING

at all the diseases that people receive from having multiple partners. And think of the suffering of the children don't have a good home life, just because of someone's idea of fun. Those kinds of thoughtless actions are disrespectful, first to God; second, to the person who committed those acts; third, to the other person; and fourth, to the child. Lack of using the gift of understanding and lack of responsibility cause so much suffering that could be avoided if we really reflected on our long-term and short-term choices. Every choice has consequences, and every decision has an end result.

Reflect on your life an hour ago, a day ago, and a year ago. Who were you with and what did you share with that person? Did you use understanding? I really believe that we often look, but don't listen. Some are only concerned about physical beauty and only look at a person on the outside. Take off the outer skin and really look at people. What are they on the inside? Try to understand them from that level.

Take time to reflect on your life—to receive understanding about who you are and what you are doing. Close your eyes and listen. You can see without even looking. Our God is understanding. Go to your room or your private space and take some time in the morning or at midday or in the evening to meditate on the Words of God. Reflect on the verses that speak to you the most. Ask for understaning and God will pour it out.

THE FEAR OF THE LORD IS WISDOM

Conversations with God

ME: How do I seek wisdom?

GOD: Look at the book of James.

James, a servant of God and of the Lord Jesus Christ, to the twelve tribes which are scattered abroad, greeting.

My brethren, count it all joy when ye fall into divers temptations; Knowing *this,* that the trying of your faith worketh patience. But let patience have her perfect work, that ye may be perfect and entire, wanting nothing. *If any of you lack wisdom, let him ask of God, that giveth to all men liberally, and upbraideth not; and it shall be given him.* But let him ask in faith, nothing wavering. For he that wavereth is like a wave of the sea driven with the wind and tossed. For let not that man think that he shall receive any thing of the Lord. A double minded man *is* unstable in all his ways. (James 1:5-8)

GOD: Now look at Solomon's example:

In Gibeon, the LORD appeared to Solomon in a dream by night: and God said, Ask what I shall give thee. And Solomon said, Thou hast shewed unto thy servant David my father great mercy, according as he walked before thee in truth, and in righteousness, and in uprightness of heart with thee; and thou hast kept for him this great kindness, that

UNDERSTANDING

thou hast given him a son to sit on his throne, as it is this day. And now, O LORD my God, thou hast made thy servant king instead of David my father: and I am but a little child: I know not how to go out or come in. And thy servant is in the midst of thy people which thou hast chosen, a great people, that cannot be numbered nor counted for multitude. Give therefore thy servant an understanding heart to judge thy people, that I may discern between good and bad: for who is able to judge this thy so great a people? And the speech pleased the Lord, that Solomon had asked this thing. And God said unto him, Because thou hast asked this thing, and hast not asked for thyself long life; neither hast asked riches for thyself, nor hast asked the life of thine enemies; but hast asked for thyself understanding to discern judgment; Behold, I have done according to thy words: lo, I have given thee a wise and an understanding heart; so that there was none like thee before thee, neither after thee shall any arise like unto thee. And I have also given thee that which thou hast not asked, both riches, and honour: so that there shall not be any among the kings like unto thee all *thy days.* And if thou wilt walk in my ways, to keep my statutes and my commandments, as thy father David did walk, then I will lengthen thy days. And Solomon awoke; and, behold, it was a dream. And he came to Jerusalem, and stood before the ark of the covenant of the LORD, and offered up burnt offerings, and offered peace offerings, and made a feast to all his servants. (1 Kings 3:5-14)

THE FEAR OF THE LORD IS WISDOM

Wisdom from the Scripture

Then shalt thou understand the fear of the LORD, and find the knowledge of God. For the LORD giveth wisdom: out of his mouth *cometh* knowledge and understanding. He layeth up sound wisdom for the righteous: *he is* a buckler to them that walk uprightly. He keepeth the paths of judgment, and preserveth the way of his saints. Then shalt thou understand righteousness, and judgment, and equity; *yea*, every good path. (Reference)

Wisdom Reflections

13

SOLITUDE

[Wisdom] *is* a tree of life to them that lay hold upon her:
and happy *is every one* that retaineth her.

—PROVERBS 3:18

Silence and solitude are necessary in developing understanding. You must have both to study the Word of God. Study with a desire to understand His Words and principles and keep an open heart to hear what He says. You will find God only if you seek him with a sincere heart.

Think on the will, laws, and commandments of God. Learn to control yourself and to listen and not speak while in conversation with God. Close your eyes and really listen. You can almost feel God's Words in your soul. Learning to listen is very important to God. I await wisdom day and night. You must be willing to go down the path of silence—to learn to just be there in the moment instead of reacting to people, places, or events. Many times I have had desires to react to what is being said to me, but it is always better to listen than to talk. Why do you think God gave us two ears and one

THE FEAR OF THE LORD IS WISDOM

mouth? Take your time. Ask God to help you resist talking and learn to listen. This will help you in every aspect of your life—with your family, children, spouse, and friends.

Listening is a very powerful tool in the way of understanding. When you are conversing with someone and you don't seem to understand, ask yourself what part of the conversation you don't understand. What are you paying attention to? Then ask, "Is it all a problem or just a piece of the problem?" Stop and reflect on it. Apply yourself to research and ask others who might have had a similar problem. Most of all, pray day and night on it. Being humble before God it is the most important attitude to have. God loves to work in people who are humble. The key is to listen to God, and be quiet in your thoughts and words. Silence is the key to listening.

Understanding involves a lot of soul searching and asking for forgiveness through Jesus Christ. You must admit to yourself that you don't have all the answers. It can be painful to reflect on the negative choices of your past. Come humbly to the Lord and ask Him to help you.

Consider you future and ask, "Who am I? Where do I want to go? What have I accomplished and what do I want to accomplish?" Often, to get to the path of understanding, you begin by walking. In my case, it was crawling. Discover what you don't like about yourself and reflect on those key behaviors. How have they negatively impacted you and how would your life be different right now if you changed them? Realize that you can't change on your own and ask God to help you. *God understands* you. Even though we don't always understand Him, His ways are higher than our ways.

14

CHANGE

[Wisdom] *is* a tree of life to them that lay hold upon her: and happy *is every one* that retaineth her.

—PROVERBS 3:18

Consider how you spend your time, money, and resources. What are your goals physically, financially, spiritually, and emotionally? How do you plan to attain those goals? Have you set out a plan with realistic deadlines and realistic expectations? You may need to change how you do things. Invest time in planning your future. Write your vision down, so you can run with it.[16] Allow your plans to be flexible with time, resources, and most of all yourself. Understanding has room for mistakes and in fact, many mistakes. We change; *God does not.* Thank God that He does not change and thank God that we can change with His help.

Life can be difficult, but God promises us that He always has a way to escape troubling times.[17] God will help you look at life and events differently. Take for instance the night of November 5, 2006. While on duty, I was involved with a subject who injured me and he was also severely injured. Initially the call went out as routine, although nothing in police work is routine. I arrived and found a naked man in an alley screaming and in a great deal of emotional pain. He was on drugs and dangerous. Drugs have can have a very dramatic impact on the body. He was Tased repeatedly and did not fall down even after being Tased eight times. In the end, he was shot and his left leg was injured. I still remember that day, November 5, 2006, 8:15 a.m. There are moments in your life that can change everything. My question for you is, how do those moments change you—for better or worse? I have a scar on my right hand. I had to have surgery on my hand, and my hand will never be the same; but then again, I will never be the same. I have learned so much about life and myself from that incident. We need God. Without Christ in our lives we are so far away from hope. The scar on my right hand honestly reminds me of where I have been and where I was in life—where my walk with the Lord was and where God wants to take me. Every journey with God is private. It's your journey with Him—the great God. He loves and cares for you, but you must be willing to change for Him.

A TIME FOR EVERYTHING

To every *thing there is* a season, and a time to every purpose under the heaven: A time to be born, and a time to die; a time to

CHANGE

plant, and a time to pluck up *that which is* planted; A time to kill, and a time to heal; a time to break down, and a time to build up; A time to weep, and a time to laugh; a time to mourn, and a time to dance; A time to cast away stones, and a time to gather stones together; a time to embrace, and a time to refrain from embracing; A time to get, and a time to lose; a time to keep, and a time to cast away; A time to rend, and a time to sew; a time to keep silence, and a time to speak; A time to love, and a time to hate; a time of war, and a time of peace. What profit hath he that worketh in that wherein he laboureth? I have seen the travail, which God hath given to the sons of men to be exercised in it.

He hath made every *thing* beautiful in his time: also he hath set the world in their heart, so that no man can find out the work that God maketh from the beginning to the end. I know that *there is* no good in them, but for *a man* to rejoice, and to do good in his life. And also that every man should eat and drink, and enjoy the good of all his labour, it *is* the gift of God. I know that, whatsoever God doeth, it shall be for ever: nothing can be put to it, nor any thing taken from it: and God doeth *it*, that *men* should fear before him. That which hath been is now; and that which is to be hath already been; and God requireth that which is past.

And moreover, I saw under the sun the place of judgment, *that* wickedness *was* there; and the place of righteousness, *that* iniquity *was* there. I said in mine heart, God shall judge the righteous and the wicked: for *there is* a time there for every purpose and for every work. I said in mine heart concerning the estate of the sons of men, that God might manifest them, and that they might see that they themselves

THE FEAR OF THE LORD IS WISDOM

are beasts. For that which befalleth the sons of men befalleth beasts; even one thing befalleth them: as the one dieth, so dieth the other; yea, they have all one breath; so that a man hath no preeminence above a beast: for all *is* vanity. All go unto one place; all are of the dust, and all turn to dust again. Who knoweth the spirit of man that goeth upward, and the spirit of the beast that goeth downward to the earth? Wherefore I perceive that *there is* nothing better, than that a man should rejoice in his own works; for that *is* his portion: for who shall bring him to see what shall be after him? (Ecclesiastes 3:1-22)

Wisdom Reflections

15

EVALUATE

[Wisdom] *is* a tree of life to them that lay hold upon her: and happy *is every one* that retaineth her.

—PROVERBS 3:18

In your search for wisdom and understanding, there are times when you need to really evaluate where you are in your life. What path have you been on the last year, month, day, or even the hours of your life? Where are you going, and how are you getting there? Where will you end up? You may not know the exact answers to these questions but they are important to ask and they are general things that you can start working toward every day.

Everybody seems to want to be rich, successful, a star, *but how?* What mode of transportation are you using every day to achieve your dreams? How fast or slow are you going in your life right now? Which direction do you want to go? Are you in a place that makes you feel happy? Where are you right now in life? Are you happy with yourself? Have you achieved all that you wanted, or do you want more? The answer often seems to be, "I want more," but the how is

THE FEAR OF THE LORD IS WISDOM

usually the problem—the right opportunity, the right venture, and meeting the right people. Be proactive with your goals. Networking is a great way to meet others in your field or in the field that you want to get into. See if there are books or associations, meetings, courses, or activities that you can get involved with to help give you exposure in the area that you are interested. If you are passionate about politics, join a political group. If you love music, get involved in your church worship program. But I also suggest you really look into it before you commit yourself; later you may regret it.

I have had a few jobs where I was just miserable, and I have seen others in the same place. They were unhappy and it affected every part of their life. Evaluate your goals and where you are in your life. You spend at least forty plus hours a week at work, and that's a lot of time to be unhappy. Are you going anywhere in your organization? Look at your date of hire and see how much you have accomplished in that time. Be honest. Did you go to school while you worked or were in involved in activities to help you grow as a person? Understanding is a beautiful gift, especially when you apply it to yourself. Maybe you feel great about where you are but if not, maybe it's time for a change.

If you know you are not where you should be, turn to God. He's there ready to direct you. When you turn to Him, he'll say, "Its okay, we can start over. I know you failed, but with Me, there is another chance." God can restore your soul and spirit for living. Even when all the chips are down, God says, "I Am right here and always have been." When you feel like no one cares, God is there. Seek God. Let Him know you are sorry you have done so little with your life. You can tell him if there are things you are not proud of. God will say,

EVALUATE

"Let's move on." Learn from your mistakes and take the good with bad. Apply yourself to understanding. Apply yourself to seeking God's direction. Let him know if you are hurting.

Sometimes life can throw you fast one—a ball so big and fast you don't think you can catch it. That's okay; God is bigger than anything life throws you. His hands are more than enough for any ball. Let go and give it to God.

We all have secret pains and issues we are not proud of—things that have happened to us we are ashamed of. I have a favorite piece of art, a small picture of Spiderman. It was created by my friend and I bought it at the opening of his gallery. That piece spoke to me; it's Spiderman curled up in a corner almost crying. It reminded me of the times I have misused the gifts God gave me to glorify Him. All of us have our own portrait of shame or our own human stain. If you will look at what you have done in the past—things said out of anger and rage or jealousy or just plain stupidity—remember that God grants you so many chances to come back to Him. We can't count as high as His mercy, but you must be sincere and fight the urge to sin because sin separates you from God.

Evaluate your life. Are there any sins that are keeping you from the fullness of His presence? What motivated you to break God's laws and when you broke them, how did you feel? Don't let sin stop you from communicating with God. God loves you and He is full of forgiveness. Please understand that He sent His only son to die for you. Do not throw away the opportunity and gift to be a child of God. Understanding the big picture of your life changes everything.

THE FEAR OF THE LORD IS WISDOM

ETERNAL LIFE

These words spake Jesus, and lifted up his eyes to heaven, and said, Father, the hour is come; glorify thy Son, that thy Son also may glorify thee: As thou hast given him power over all flesh, that he should give eternal life to as many as thou hast given him. And this is life eternal, that they might know thee the only true God, and Jesus Christ, whom thou hast sent. I have glorified thee on the earth: I have finished the work which thou gavest me to do. And now, O Father, glorify thou me with thine own self with the glory which I had with thee before the world was. (John 17:1-5)

ME: What is love?

GOD: I Am.

Now before the feast of the Passover, when Jesus knew that his hour was come that he should depart out of this world unto the Father, having loved his own which were in the world, he loved them unto the end. And supper being ended, the devil having now put into the heart of Judas

EVALUATE

Iscariot, Simon's *son*, to betray him; Jesus knowing that the Father had given all things into his hands, and that he was come from God, and went to God; He riseth from supper, and laid aside his garments; and took a towel, and girded himself. After that he poureth water into a bason, and began to wash the disciples' feet, and to wipe *them* with the towel wherewith he was girded. Then cometh he to Simon Peter: and Peter saith unto him, Lord, dost thou wash my feet? Jesus answered and said unto him, what I do thou knowest not now; but thou shalt know hereafter. Peter saith unto him, Thou shalt never wash my feet. Jesus answered him, If I wash thee not, thou hast no part with me. Simon Peter saith unto him, Lord, not my feet only, but also *my* hands and *my* head. Jesus saith to him, He that is washed needeth not save to wash *his* feet, but is clean every whit: and ye are clean, but not all. For he knew who should betray him; therefore said he, Ye are not all clean. So after he had washed their feet, and had taken his garments, and was set down again, he said unto them, Know ye what I have done to you? Ye call me Master and Lord: and ye say well; for *so* I am. If I then, *your* Lord and Master, have washed your feet; ye also ought to wash one another's feet. For I have given you an example, that ye should do as I have done to you. Verily, verily, I say unto you, the servant is not greater than his lord; neither he that is sent greater than he that sent him. If ye know these things, happy are ye if ye do them. (John 13: 1-17)

Jesus said, Now is the Son of man glorified, and God is glorified in him. If God be glorified in him, God shall also glorify him in himself, and shall straightway glorify him. Little children, yet a little while I am with you. Ye shall seek me: and as I said unto the Jews, Whither I go, ye cannot

THE FEAR OF THE LORD IS WISDOM

come; so now I say to you. A new commandment I give unto you, that ye love one another; as I have loved you, that ye also love one another. By this shall all *men* know that ye are my disciples, if ye have love one to another. (John 13:31-35)

Wisdom Reflections

16

WISDOM TO SERVE

[Wisdom] *is* a tree of life to them that lay hold upon her:
and happy *is every one* that retaineth her.

—PROVERBS 3:18

I find it difficult at times to do my Christian work. I get tired and worn out, so sometimes I come home and light the candles and just relax in God's arms. I find rest in His peace and in God's private space created just for me. I take a hot shower and I ask God to give me the peace that passes all understanding. There is no spa, vacation, or resort that can compare to Him. I have been to some very nice resorts with my wife, and nothing compares to just five minutes with my Lord. Jesus said, "Take my yoke upon you and learn of me; for I am meek and lowly in heart: and ye shall find rest unto your souls." (Matthew 11:29).

Jesus knew life could be difficult and at times we would lose sight of our prize. The Apostle Paul said, "Stay focused on your prize, run the race of faith" [Reference]. In addition to your reward in heaven, you will also receive a prize. Nothing is better than heaven and being with the Lord Jesus, but He wants to give all of us rewards as well as heaven and being with Him. That's how generous Jesus is. Christ wants more for you than even you want for yourself. Stay focused on the prize—the great commission of Christ, the work he has assigned to you and me. Always stay focused on the mission, your private assignment for God. Keep your eyes on Christ. You will be rewarded in ways we cannot understand. There are five crowns listed in the Bible: (1) crown of life, (2) crown of righteousness, (3) crown of incorruptibility, (4) crown of glory, and (5) crown of rejoicing.

This does not mean he cannot or will not create a special crown just for you; there are gifts, treasures, and wonders that are for you and only you. You will be rewarded for what you have done for Christ and for the Gospel. God has his own special Santa bag, and believe me, he has kept a list of who has been naughty and nice—who is a lukewarm Christian or a Christian of true service and has works to back it up. Do everything in your way to honor God, to serve God. Not everyone is called for the same thing or the same type of service but we are all called by God to serve.

CALLED BY GOD

And the LORD spoke unto Moses, saying, See, I have called by name Bezaleel the son of Uri, the son of Hur, of

WISDOM TO SERVE

the tribe of Judah: *And I have filled him with the spirit of God, in wisdom, and in understanding, and in knowledge, and in all manner of workmanship,* To devise cunning works, to work in gold, and in silver, and in brass, And in cutting of stones, to set *them*, and in carving of timber, to work in all manner of workmanship. And I, behold, I have given with him Aholiab, the son of Ahisamach, of the tribe of Dan: and in the hearts of all that are wise hearted I have put wisdom, that they may make all that I have commanded thee; The tabernacle of the congregation, and the ark of the testimony, and the mercy seat that *is* thereupon, and all the furniture of the tabernacle, And the table and his furniture, and the pure candlestick with all his furniture, and the altar of incense, And the altar of burnt offering with all his furniture, and the laver and his foot, And the cloths of service, and the holy garments for Aaron the priest, and the garments of his sons, to minister in the priest's office, And the anointing oil, and sweet incense for the holy *place*: according to all that I have commanded thee shall they do. (Exodus 31:1-11)

Conversations with God

ME: I love this, what does it mean?

The LORD said unto my Lord, Sit thou at my right hand, until I make thine enemies thy footstool. The LORD shall send the rod of thy strength out of Zion: rule thou in the midst of thine enemies. Thy people *shall be* willing in the day of thy power, in the beauties of holiness from the womb

THE FEAR OF THE LORD IS WISDOM

of the morning: thou hast the dew of thy youth. *The LORD hath sworn, and will not repent; Thou art a priest for ever after the order of Melchizedek.*

The Lord at thy right hand shall strike through kings in the day of his wrath. He shall judge among the heathen, he shall fill *the places* with the dead bodies; he shall wound the heads over many countries. He shall drink of the brook in the way: therefore shall he lift up the head. (Psalms 110: 1-7)

GOD: You will be with me forever.

ME: What about different spirits or gifts of the spirit?

GOD: "And there shall come forth a rod out of the stem of Jesse, and a Branch shall grow out of his roots: And the spirit of the LORD shall rest upon him, the spirit of wisdom and understanding, the spirit of counsel and might, the spirit of knowledge and of the fear of the LORD;

"And in that day thou shalt say, O LORD, I will praise thee: though thou wast angry with me, thine anger is turned away, and thou comfortedst me. Behold, God is my salvation; I will trust, and not be afraid: for the LORD JEHOVAH is my strength and my song; he is my god" (Isaiah 11:1-2).

Wisdom Reflections

17

IMPACT

[Wisdom] *is* a tree of life to them that lay hold upon her:
and happy *is every one* that retaineth her.

—PROVERBS 3:18

Consider the path of your life, your journey. Where will it take you? Where will you be in five or ten years from now? What kind of home will you live in and what kind of car will you drive? How much time did you donate to church or give to God? How did you help spread the Word of God? How much have you given to the cause of God, which is to save that which is and was lost? How much of your time, how much of your money, and how much of yourself did you give to God? Every day you can make a change, a difference in your life, and in your community. You can have an impact that can change the world. By one man, Adam, sin entered the world, and by one man, Jesus Christ, salvation came to the world. Salvation is the greatest impact on any person. What are you doing to create an impact for God?

THE FEAR OF THE LORD IS WISDOM

People say they are only one person. What can they do? How much of a difference can one person have? How much difference can I make? You can start with you, then your family, your work, and your community. Take time to consider: all great ideas, goals, or visions start with just one person. They share their ideas and visions with other people and often years later, that idea or vision becomes a beautiful reality with the help of others.

Please remember, it's a long path, but stay on it. Do not allow yourself to be distracted or taken off course. Keep your feet on the ground and stay focused. Stay planted in your place of destiny and in your path of understanding. Understanding allows you to see, hear, and feel how things really are and how they should be.

I recall many times when I have been dispatched to a domestic violence call. The citizens involved think the police can handle everything. Many people do not realize that some officers are not married or do not have children. They may not have enough life experience to understand what is really going on. To make matters worse, the public has an expectation for the police to be like knights in shining armor. When we arrive, we only know what the dispatcher has told us. If I were not married with kids, how could I understand family life and the repercussions of a domestic dispute? I may have some experience with a family, but it may be totally different than the situation I am going into. For example, I have no sisters or brothers and I never knew my father. In some ways I am lost as to what a traditional family is; it's almost alien to me. How am I supposed to fix their problems? I need understanding from God. In your life, you need understanding from God because you just don't know everything about everyone. In order to have the greatest impact, you need to follow God's wisdom.

Conversations with God

ME: What is true wisdom and knowledge?

GOD: Me and *only* Me.

For the preaching of the cross is to them that perish foolishness; but unto us which are saved it is the power of God. For it is written, I will destroy the wisdom of the wise, and will bring to nothing the understanding of the prudent. Where is the wise? Where is the scribe? Where is the disputer of this world? Hath not God made foolish the wisdom of this world? For after that in the wisdom of God the world by wisdom knew not God, it pleased God by the foolishness of preaching to save them that believe. For the Jews require a sign, and the Greeks seek after wisdom: But we preach Christ crucified, unto the Jews a stumblingblock, and unto the Greeks foolishness; But unto them which are called, both Jews and Greeks, Christ the power of God, and the wisdom of God. Because the foolishness of God is wiser than men; and the weakness of God is stronger than men. For ye see your calling, brethren, how that not many wise men after the flesh, not many mighty, not many noble, are called: But God hath chosen the foolish things of the world to confound the wise; and God hath chosen the weak things of the world to confound the things which are mighty; And base things of the world, and things which are despised,

THE FEAR OF THE LORD IS WISDOM

hath God chosen, yea, and things which are not, to bring to nought things that are: That no flesh should glory in his presence. But of him are ye in Christ Jesus, who of God is made unto us wisdom, and righteousness, and sanctification, and redemption: That, according as it is written, He that glorieth, let him glory in the Lord. (1 Corinthians 1:18-31)

ME: What are forms of worldly wisdom?

GOD: Who is Wise among you?

Who *is* the wise man who may understand this? And *who is he* to whom the mouth of the LORD has spoken, that he may declare it? Why does the land perish *and* burn up like a wilderness, so that no one can pass through? And the LORD said, "Because they have forsaken My law which I set before them, and have not obeyed My voice, nor walked according to it, but they have walked according to the dictates of their own hearts and after the Baals, which their fathers taught them," therefore thus says the LORD of hosts, the God of Israel: "Behold, I will feed them, this people, with wormwood, and give them water of gall to drink. I will scatter them also among the Gentiles, whom neither they nor their fathers have known. And I will send a sword after them until I have consumed them."

Thus says the LORD: "Let not the wise *man* glory in his wisdom, let not the mighty *man* glory in his might, nor let the rich *man* glory in his riches; but let him who glories glory in this, That he understands and knows Me, That I *am* the LORD, exercising lovingkindness, judgment, and righteousness in the earth. For in these I delight," says the LORD. (Jeremiah 9:12-16, 22-24 NKJV)

Wisdom Reflections

18

COMPASSION

[Wisdom] *is* a tree of life to them that lay hold upon her: and happy *is every one* that retaineth her.

—PROVERBS 3:18

Understanding and compassion are both mentioned in the Scripture and they have many similarities, yet they are different. Understanding is the ability to understand, comprehend, and realize the situation individually and then as a whole. Understanding is the ability to see future consequences or results, look at each component of the situation separately, and then put it back together. Understanding sees how each part interacts with the other parts to make a whole.

Compassion is more emotional and sympathetic of the end result, and if you don't help that person or take care of their situation, there will be a negative and profound outcome. Understanding is both logical and emotional, but much more logical in the sense of being able to reason and assess the situation, the person, and the problem.

THE FEAR OF THE LORD IS WISDOM

The Bible tells us that when Jesus was moved with compassion, many people were healed and set free. He was also full of understanding and understanding itself. We have the capacity for both understanding and compassion because we get both from God. You do receive some level of understanding from education, study, reading, and life experiences, but the ultimate understanding comes from God. There is no understanding that can compare or compete with God's understanding for God is understanding; he can see right through our thoughts. He knows what kind of choices we will make and the consequences of those choices on the rest of our lives. The Creator of the universe knows all before it happens and sees everything at the same time. He is not bound by space or time. That is hard for us to grasp, but it also gives us perspective on the vastness of his wisdom and understanding.

There is no escape from God's eyes or ears. Your deepest thoughts, desires, and secrets are open and known to him. But since He is full of compassion for you, there is safety in Him. You can be open and vulnerable before Him.

Wisdom Reflections

19

THINK

[Wisdom] *is* a tree of life to them that lay hold upon her: and happy *is every one* that retaineth her.

—PROVERBS 3:18

What have you done or not done in your life right now that would be beneficial?

Once when I asked God for wisdom, His response was: "Look at the homeless person and what do you see?"

My response was, "A person looking for food and shelter."

His response was, "I see a soul worth saving."

Just because we see a situation in a certain way, or even our own life a certain way, does not mean that it cannot change. The power of wisdom and understanding does what the human mind cannot.

God said to seek Him day and night—to pray, talk, and even sing to Him—for He hears us. We are important to Him. We are the apple of His eye. Our God is amazing. He is looking at you, me,

THE FEAR OF THE LORD IS WISDOM

and everyone at the same time—seeing, listening, and thinking about what we will do next. I ask God for wisdom every chance I get, but I have failed many times, committing sin after sin after sin. I asked God, "Why is it so difficult to be good?" He answered, "Because none are, but My grace is greater." His grace motivates me to keep trying and to keep seeking His wisdom.

I asked God, "Why is the world the way it is?"

God replied, "Think on this: Many times people are in their situation because of the way they think, react, and feel toward themselves and life."

Your thoughts, words, deeds, and actions have a dramatic impact on your life. Consider what you think about. How do you view the aspects of your life and the world around you? Then notice how others think differently than you. Ask yourself what separates you from them. Is it the way you think, how you feel, your values, your method of thinking, and your approach to life? Think on how you interpret a situation. These are all factors that affect whether you think in a positive way or a negative way, and that affects your outcome.

It's easy to say that all the bad in the world is God's fault, but consider the human race. We need to reflect on our morals, our values, and our way of thinking. We are so quick to point to God. What about us? Where are we in the equation? Where do we fit in? Are we not free to think, feel, and act? Should we not hold ourselves accountable for our behavior and how we react to the events in our lives? Many times, we want to put God on trial, but what about you?

THINK

Try cross-examining yourself, your life, your ways of thinking, and your way of reacting to life.

What if you made a checklist or a diary of the good things you do and the bad. You could even create a point system! It would give you a guide and a glimpse of the real you and how you behave. Write down how you relate to people at work, how you greet your coworkers, how you treated your spouse, or your boss, how you said hello or good-bye to your kids or parents. Think about yourself. Take a self-inventory. It is okay not to be perfect in the mirror and even if it breaks, it's okay. I am still a piece of work myself. Thank God that He is *patient*.

Seek God about making a list and pray about it daily. Spend quality time with God and spend time doing God's will; it is important to spend time alone with God in prayer and in reading the living Word of God, the Bible. Ask God to give you wisdom, understanding, and counsel. Ask Him, "What can I learn from this situation or problem? Give me wisdom and understanding to resolve this situation." God can turn any negative situation for good if you bring it before Him in prayer (Romans 8:26-28).

We all have sins and challenges in life and it's how you handle them that makes the difference. Do not react to a situation immediately. Take the time to look at and assess the situation. What do you see, hear, and feel? What is that in front of you? People have a tendency to overreact, get loud, or too excited when something happens. You need to control that. Why? Because with emotion can come pure reaction and logic is better. Logic has a methodical approach that calms us down. For example, impulse buying is to buy

THE FEAR OF THE LORD IS WISDOM

something just to buy it. Later, people often return impulse items. They decide, *I really don't need that* or *I don't have the space for that or this is not what I wanted.* I have done that many times, but I'm much better than I used to be. I remember buying those nice things from TV commercials and then I had to return them. I lost both ways; the shipping was not refundable and to ship it back was just as expensive as the item. I remember the shipping bills were outrageous fees. I even bought a bed one time and it was $300 to send it back. Keep track of what you spend and you will see where it goes. Think before you leap and ask yourself, "Why do I need this?" There is so much power in that question: *Why?*

Wisdom Reflections

20

DISTRACTIONS

[Wisdom] *is* a tree of life to them that lay hold upon her:
and happy *is every one* that retaineth her.

—PROVERBS 3:18

Hosea has been called the Deathbed Prophet of Israel because he was the last to prophesy before the northern kingdom fell to Assyria (about 722 BC). His ministry followed a golden age in the northern kingdom with a peace and prosperity not seen since the days of Solomon.

Unfortunately, this prosperity led to moral decay, and Israel forsook God to worship idols. So God instructed Hosea to marry a prostitute whose unfaithfulness to her husband would serve as an example of Israel's unfaithfulness to God. Hosea then explained God's complaint against Israel and warned of the punishment that would come unless the people returned to the Lord and remained faithful to him. The book shows the depth of God's love for his people, a love that is merciful and forgiving, but also tolerates no rivals.

THE FEAR OF THE LORD IS WISDOM

Read the book of Hosea and see how God always takes us back.

Just like the idols in Hosea's time, there are idols or distractions we deal with today. When I consider all the endless hours playing video games, surfing the net, or just buying things over the Internet, I feel sad about the time, energy, and resources I could have used serving and honoring God. Think about how much you could have given. Make a personal choice to catch up. Do something every single day. Pick something and do it whether it is serving an hour at home, reading to the elderly, or serving at a hospital. There are thousands of things we can do to honor God.

How much money have we spent and not considered that we should donate to a good cause? Before you donate a penny, find out about the charity. Do your homework. It's important. Search and ask God for wisdom to make the right donation in all aspects whether it is time or money. After you have confirmation from God, start to give in some way every day—as much as you can, even if it is just one hour. You may think that an hour is too much. Tell me what you are really doing with your time. Look at your schedule, write it down, and reflect. Are you spending too much time shopping in the mall for things you don't need? Are you doing anything productive at all?

Ask yourself what pays the best dividends and return for your time. If it furthers God's kingdom, the rewards are great. You will always get more than 100 percent back guaranteed. Invest in the best, most secure bank in the universe with the best rewards and returns possible on earth and in heaven. God's kingdom is open seven days a week, twenty-four hours a day. He is your reward and

DISTRACTIONS

when you have Him, you have all you need. What you desire is nothing compared to God and His love for you. You may take care of family members or someone who is sick and feel you can't make the time. Then do the best with whom you're with. That is honor to God. Raise your children in a Christian home and set the example for a Christian lifestyle. Keep your life centered on Christ. Why? Because He came to earth for that very reason—to save us, teach us, and show us God's mercy, love, and compassion for us. Why can't we do the same for our Lord and Master? Why can't we offer some of our time and money? We can sacrifice for the One who gave up all so we could have all. We were not God's children until Christ invited us to the family through His death and resurrection. Always remember He gave first and gave all, everything. His pain is our pleasure; He died so we could live.

JESUS ULTIMATE SACRIFICE

And Pilate wrote a title, and put *it* on the cross. And the writing was, JESUS OF NAZARETH THE KING OF THE JEWS. This title then read many of the Jews: for the place where Jesus was crucified was nigh to the city: and it was written in Hebrew, *and* Greek, *and* Latin. Then said the chief priests of the Jews to Pilate, Write not, The King of the Jews; but that he said, I am King of the Jews. Pilate answered, What I have written I have written. Then the soldiers, when they had crucified Jesus, took his garments, and made four parts, to every soldier a part; and also *his* coat: now the coat was without seam, woven from the top throughout. They said therefore among themselves, Let us not rend it, but cast lots for it, whose it shall be: that the scripture might be fulfilled, which saith, They parted my raiment among them, and for my vesture they did cast lots. These things therefore the soldiers did. Now there stood by the cross of Jesus his mother, and his mother's sister, Mary the *wife* of Cleophas, and Mary Magdalene. When Jesus therefore saw his mother, and the disciple standing by, whom he loved, he saith unto his mother, Woman, behold thy son! Then saith he to the disciple, Behold thy mother! And from that hour that disciple took her unto his own *home*. After this, Jesus knowing that all things were now accomplished, that the scripture might be fulfilled, saith, I thirst. Now there was set a vessel full of vinegar: and they filled a spunge with vinegar, and put *it* upon hyssop, and put *it* to his mouth. When Jesus therefore had received the vinegar, he said, *It is finished: and he bowed his head, and gave up the ghost.* (John 19:19-30)

Wisdom Reflections

21

THOUGHTS

[Wisdom] *is* a tree of life to them that lay hold upon her:
and happy *is every one* that retaineth her.

—PROVERBS 3:18

I know I feel troubled because of my ill grandfather. You can't imagine how hard it's been for me, seeing him dying a little bit every day—losing his memory, his ability to function. He has been bedridden for over nine months. It started with depression about three years ago and eventually it consumed him. If any of you have sick loved ones, which I am sure you do, my heart goes out to you. It's been one of the hardest things I have had to accept and deal with. We have tried everything, and yet nothing has changed.

How you feel about yourself, others, and events have traumatic impact on your life. How you see yourself affects you in every way—in your career, your love, your emotions, your physical health, your spiritual life, your social life, everything. Your thoughts toward yourself have power. Monitor your thoughts. Be careful what you focus on, and think about it. I can tell you from firsthand experience

THE FEAR OF THE LORD IS WISDOM

that how we see things impacts us at every level. Notice if your thoughts are good or bad. Do you say positive or negative things? Are you supportive or destructive? Do people like being around you or avoid you? Do people like or dislike you and why? Ask yourself this question, "How do others view me?" Why do some people get smiles and hellos and others good-bye? "Sorry, I have to go" or "Can't make it" or "I am busy," are responses that can be hurtful, but they can reveal something about the way you think and the things you talk about. Let God help you with your thoughts. Try to think like He does in His Word. He is always positive and always looking out for your good.

Many times God wants you to just learn to trust in him. God is there in all the good, bad, and ugly. Explain to God your pain, your hurt, your sorrow. It's okay to cry in front of God. Get on your knees and bow your head. Ask for forgiveness if your situation is a result of sin. If not, still kneel and bow your head and tell God, "I am right here hurting right now. I can't do this, Father, without you." I have had days, weeks, and months like that. I spent almost two years like that. It was a difficult time, but God had a plan; He always does. It was a bad situation, but He turned it for my good. I learned to seek Him and know Him, to understand that He is the one true God (through our Lord Jesus Christ.) Seek God with a humble heart. God won't hide himself. He loves a humble person.

THOUGHTS

Wisdom from the Scriptures
THE HOLY SPIRIT

Verily, verily, I say unto you, He that believeth on me, the works that I do shall he do also; and greater *works* than these shall he do; because I go unto my Father. And whatsoever ye shall ask in my name, that will I do, that the Father may be glorified in the Son. If ye shall ask any thing in my name, I will do *it*.

If ye love me, keep my commandments. And I will pray the Father, and he shall give you another Comforter, that he may abide with you for ever; *Even* the Spirit of truth; whom the world cannot receive, because it seeth him not, neither knoweth him: but ye know him; for he dwelleth with you, and shall be in you.

I will not leave you comfortless: I will come to you. Yet a little while, and the world seeth me no more; but ye see me: because I live, ye shall live also. At that day ye shall know that I am in my Father, and ye in me, and I in you. He that hath my commandments, and keepeth them, he it is that loveth me: and he that loveth me shall be loved of my Father, and I will love him, and will manifest myself to him. Judas saith unto him, not Iscariot, Lord, how is it that thou wilt manifest thyself unto us, and not unto the world? Jesus answered and said unto him, If a man love me, he will keep my words: and my Father will love him, and we will come unto him, and make our abode with him. He that loveth me

THE FEAR OF THE LORD IS WISDOM

not keepeth not my sayings: and the word which ye hear is not mine, but the Father's which sent me.

These things have I spoken unto you, being *yet* present with you. But the Comforter, *which is* the Holy Ghost, whom the Father will send in my name, he shall teach you all things, and bring all things to your remembrance, whatsoever I have said unto you. Peace I leave with you, my peace I give unto you: not as the world giveth, give I unto you. Let not your heart be troubled, neither let it be afraid. (John 14:12-27)

Wisdom Reflections

22

THE GIFT

[Wisdom] *is* a tree of life to them that lay hold upon her:
and happy *is every one* that retaineth her.

—PROVERBS 3:18

I remember I was asking God for a certain gift, and God said to me, "Is that all you seek Me for? Do you not want My love or Me, for I Am your great and exceeding reward?" God is the ultimate reward.

God is both the giver and the gift. If was asked if I could have anything in the world, I would choose an intimate relationship with Jesus Christ, my Lord and savior. It is important to pray every day, and you will have your own special prayers just like I did and you will find your own private needs met. But don't stop there. Always seek wisdom, understanding, and counsel from God. It makes the path of life not only possible but also incredibly beyond what you can imagine.

God is a gift to us and we are to be a blessing to others. Watch your actions. Don't do things unless you know there will be positive

THE FEAR OF THE LORD IS WISDOM

results. For example, don't change things that affect other people unless you talk it over with them. Get their feedback and find out how they feel about your decision. Learn to get the "we" instead of the "me." Resist the temptation to do things only to please yourself. A wise person resists temptations, even flees the situation in order not to be tempted or fall into sin. If the sin is not present or around you, then most likely you will not sin. Do not invite sin through your front door to see how strong you are for I tell you, you will fall flat on your face. Do not think that you are immune to sin now that you are a child of God. Remember, only Christ was sinless. Please use caution, and do not go to war without the armor of God for you will lose.[18] Think and meditate on the Bible. Write down and highlight your favorite passages and books or even go to Bible study. I did and it was very interesting. Go to church to worship with others; it is essential to a Christian life. Discuss your questions one-on-one with a pastor or elder. Find a mentor to help explain the Scriptures to you so that it may be clearer. I highly recommend purchasing a Bible study guide. If you have a favorite book of the Bible or certain topic, you can find individual study courses. It will provide a tremendous amount of clarity and you will enjoy the Word of God even more. Develop your Christian life so that you can be a gift to others.

Be on your guard against gossip. It's deceptive and hurtful. If a fellow Christian comes to gossip or talk about others, ask yourself three questions:

1. What does God think about what this person is saying?
2. Is what this person saying positive or negative?
3. Is what this person saying true or false?

THE GIFT

Avoid gossip at all costs. If a Christian or non-Christian comes to talk to you, do not run around and tell others about that person's problems or situation. Be a true friend and try to help them. Pray with them, invite them to church, or if they give you permission, seek others to help them. Do not turn a chance or opportunity to serve God into a chance to serve Satan.

Always be encouraging and try to be a Christian in every aspect of your life—work, sports, home, and with friends and family. We are God's children 24/7. You do not stop being a father or a mother or a son or daughter. We are always and foremost Christian children of God. Our walk with God should reflect this in every aspect of our lives. What would Jesus do? Ask yourself what you have done for Jesus. What does the Lord think of what you are doing in your life right now—every day, every hour? The fact that you are reading this book shows that you are seeking Him.

Consider how you spend your time. Is it glorifying Christ or being selfish? Evaluate your life and determine if you are being a blessing to God and to others. Does your life please God? And what can you do to change right now? You must accept Christ if you have not already. You must repent and you must accept and receive the Holy Spirit. Then pray, "God, what mission do You have for me in life? What can I do to glorify You?" God can use you in ways you can't even imagine. He will empower you with skills and talents that you weren't even aware that you had. God will show you how to use what you already have for His purpose and for His will. Nothing is impossible to God—nothing. God is the great Creator, Redeemer, and above all, He loves and cherishes you.

THE FEAR OF THE LORD IS WISDOM

My prayer for you is this: *may the God of love grant you your deepest wishes and desires in this life and the next. May your life be a glory to and for God, and may you seek God in all things and at all times and in all ways. May Jesus be the Lord of your life.*

I think about my race for the prize in Christ day and night. Consider the prize God gives to those who are faithful; He gives more than you can even ask for in this life and the next. So when things get tough and you don't feel like going to church, who do you really think you are cheating? Is God not the gift and the giver of greatest gifts in this life and the next? Invest in yourself. Give your time, your heart, your soul, your body, and as much as you can financially to support the things that are Christ-driven to spread the truth of the Gospel of Christ or to help the poor and the needy. Donate what you don't need. You receive two benefits: your home looks cleaner and bigger, and you just made God smile at you even more. Donate those shoes, purses, pants, socks, anything and everything you don't need. I can promise that someone needs it more than you. It really hurts me to see people throw away food or items that have value. Donate it. I have done some things—crazy things to donate for a good cause, but that's between God and me. He keeps a list. Don't you want to have many pages in His good book? Make it your goal that God actually gets tired of counting and just says, "Okay, you can have anything." Wouldn't it be great to have God greet you face-to-face in heaven and tell you that? Christ will be our judge and the one to say whether we are a good and faithful servant. "I will give you all your rewards and prizes because of your love and obedience to me."

Wisdom Reflections

2 3

GREAT POWER

[Wisdom] *is* a tree of life to them that lay hold upon her:
and happy *is every one* that retaineth her.

—PROVERBS 3:18

There is great power in wisdom if you take the time to really explore and seek it.

When I had my knee surgery, I did not realize what I lost and what insight I had gained. It's only through wisdom one can see beyond themselves and beyond their situation. When we are in the midst of a struggle we never see the lesson and only see the pain. We don't see the power in the solitude. In those moments where you not only discover God and His power, you also discover yourself and the things and thoughts that you did not even know you had. You discover both good and bad—how you react or did not react to certain events, people, and places.

God's wisdom can overcome any and all of your problems, your issues, and your demons because of Jesus, the Lamb of God. We

THE FEAR OF THE LORD IS WISDOM

have access to God because of the Lord Jesus Christ, the son of the living God, who redeems our lives and souls. We are made whole through Him and only through Christ, our mighty Savior.

Because of Jesus, you may ask God for the power of wisdom. When you are having anger issues, God's wisdom is stronger. When you start getting upset, loud, or out of control, God's strength is stronger. There have been many times when I was about to fall into sin and felt like I was literally fighting with myself. A war was going on inside of me for my soul and my entire being. I chose God's wisdom.

Many times we feel like we are being torn between two people perhaps because of a home situation, a work situation, or a neighbor problem. Pray in Jesus' name that God will give you wisdom to overcome those situations. If you start to get nervous or uncomfortable around certain people or situations, you often don't know what to say or how to say what's needed. If there's anything to say at all, ask God. *The very power of wisdom is God because God is wisdom.* Be humble before Him and say, "God, I need some help. I am in trouble. What do I do? I don't know what to do." Allow God to take over and He will help you.

There have been times I have said, "Wow that was me," and there have been moments of failure and disgrace. There are times of strength and weakness. You can learn from both if you really apply yourself to God.

GREAT POWER

CONSIDER WISDOM'S WAY

We all want answers, but we want them our way and in our time and in our liking. Wisdom is not like that. First you must accept Christ who is the very wisdom and power of God made flesh, and after you have given him your heart and your soul, then you may proceed and ask God for wisdom, understanding, and counsel.

Ask yourself this question: what is wisdom and what can the power of wisdom allow me to do differently or see? Reflect when you are in the moment of despair. See and feel how different it is to have wisdom beside you and in you.

With wisdom comes great responsibility. With wisdom comes power, but you must be careful not to become prideful. I often think how many times I have become prideful because of wisdom. I have misused God's great and loving gift. I have blown great opportunities to share Christ with someone; instead, I just wanted to sound wise.

Wisdom always protects. It does not hurt and never reacts out of anger or hatred. It shields us from ourselves and does not act out of pride, anger, or fear. It allows us to overcome sin through Christ. I know there may be moments when you may think, *I can't do this, I am not strong enough.* That's where God says, "You can through

THE FEAR OF THE LORD IS WISDOM

Christ." God is right there with you and with Him you can overcome anything. Christ already has.

Every time you lose your temper, call on the power of God to give you wisdom to help overcome your issue or weaknesses. Ask God to give you understanding to get you through it. I know there are times when I pleaded with God and have said, "God please give me wisdom, counsel me, great Lord. Get me through this. You are my strength and shield."

God wants to get you through your hard times right now. Call the Almighty to give you the power of wisdom and the true power of understanding to get you through your trial or your great tribulation. There is nothing too difficult for God. Nothing is too hard, too big, or too difficult for God. We all have our Red Sea, our Gethsemane. God is not only willing but also able to get you through your trial. Call upon the Lord, the most High to see His power to work through you.

Paul the Apostle had a thorn in his side, and God said, "My grace is sufficient, my strength is perfect in your weakness."[19] When you think it's impossible, that's when God says, "I Am right here." Seek His face, His glory, and know the power of God in all things and at all times.

Many only search for God when things are bad or tough or difficult; chose to seek God in good times and bad times. Repent of your sins because this actually prevents the true power of God from working. Always make time for God and His glory. Spend time in church and in silence, seeking His face and His will for your life.

GREAT POWER

Wisdom from the Scriptures
GOD'S WAYS AND REWARDS

My son, forget not my law; but let thine heart keep my commandments: For length of days, and long life, and peace, shall they add to thee. Let not mercy and truth forsake thee: bind them about thy neck; write them upon the table of thine heart: So shalt thou find favour and good understanding in the sight of God and man. Trust in the LORD with all thine heart; and lean not unto thine own understanding. In all thy ways acknowledge him, and he shall direct thy paths.

Be not wise in thine own eyes: fear the LORD, and depart from evil. It shall be health to thy navel, and marrow to thy bones. Honour the LORD with thy substance, and with the firstfruits of all thine increase: So shall thy barns be filled with plenty, and thy presses shall burst out with new wine. My son, despise not the chastening of the LORD; neither be weary of his correction: For whom the LORD loveth he correcteth; even as a father the son *in whom* he delighteth.

Happy *is* the man *that* findeth wisdom, and the man *that* getteth understanding. For the merchandise of it *is* better than the merchandise of silver, and the gain thereof than fine gold. She *is* more precious than rubies: and all the things thou canst desire are not to be compared unto her. Length of days *is* in her right hand; *and* in her left hand riches and honour. Her ways *are* ways of pleasantness, and all her paths *are* peace. She *is* a tree of life to them that lay

THE FEAR OF THE LORD IS WISDOM

hold upon her: and happy *is every one* that retaineth her. The LORD by wisdom hath founded the earth; by understanding hath he established the heavens. By his knowledge the depths are broken up, and the clouds drop down the dew. (Proverbs 3:1-20)

Wisdom Reflections

24

YOUR ARMOR

> [Wisdom] *is* a tree of life to them that lay hold upon her:
> and happy *is every one* that retaineth her.
>
> —PROVERBS 3:18

We are at war with ourselves—the flesh or natural man against the spirit or spiritual man. The Bible tells us that the natural man does not like the things of the spirit and fights against them, but our spiritual man can control the natural if we stay strong in the Lord, His Word, and prayer.[20]

Ephesians 6:10-18 tells us to put on the armor of God so that we can stand against the lust of our natural man and the temptation of Satan:

> Finally, my brethren, be strong in the Lord and in the power of His might. Put on the whole armor of God, that you may be able to stand against the wiles of the devil. For we do not wrestle against flesh and blood, but against principalities, against powers, against the rulers of the darkness of this age, against spiritual *hosts* of wickedness in the

THE FEAR OF THE LORD IS WISDOM

heavenly *places*. Therefore take up the whole armor of God, that you may be able to withstand in the evil day, and having done all, to stand.

Stand therefore, having girded your waist with truth, having put on the breastplate of righteousness, and having shod your feet with the preparation of the gospel of peace; above all, taking the shield of faith with which you will be able to quench all the fiery darts of the wicked one. And take the helmet of salvation, and the sword of the Spirit, which is the word of God; praying always with all prayer and supplication in the Spirit, being watchful to this end with all perseverance and supplication for all the saints. (NKJV)

Put on the whole armor of God and when you look at your opponent, be prepared to see yourself. You are your worst enemy; you are at war with your old sinful self. Put on the armor of God and pray; ask God for strength and, above all, wisdom.

Sometimes I imagine myself with shield of fire in my left hand and in my right hand a sword of fire. This is just a way of preparing myself for war and, believe, me it is war. At times I imagine myself wearing the full armor of God like a warrior ready for battle. I remind myself that nothing is impossible to God. I am sharing with you what has helped me in those times that I was weak in hopes that it will help you as well. I ask God to give me the fire and power of wisdom and the true power of understanding. Remember there is no problem too big for God, and God will use challenges and hardship to show you His ultimate power and wisdom.

We are not to be afraid of anyone or anything save the reverence and fear of the Lord our God.[21] Only tremble at Him and His

YOUR ARMOR

Word; only fear to disobey God. But when a problem comes your way and you are caught off guard or unsure how to handle the situation, ask for God's wisdom to guide you.

When challenges come, look at God to be your shield and your strength.[22] God will not only shield you but will give you the victory. He will show you how, through Him, you can have victory, but you must stay faithful to God. You must try to behave like a child of God and not be willfully sinning or exposing your self to sin.

Through a sinful lifestyle or through association with others, you should always carry yourself like a Christian. Your friends and the people you spend time with should be Christians. Don't exclude others—not at all—but non-Christians may not understand or respect your faith. They may not have the same morals or values. There are many non-Christians and many of other faiths that are good people, but they may lead you astray. You need a core group of Christians that support you and pray for you. Unfortunately, I have met many non-Christians that act and have more ethical values then a lot of Christians that I know. Please respect other people's faith and belief.

Use your judgment and look at the commandment of God on how you are to conduct yourself daily. Look at how a Christian should live and act. Do your friends or your associates read the Bible or discuss topics of the Bible? Consider how you are spending your time with others and what kind of people you are spending time with. Are they building you up in the family of Christ or not?

If you are a in a difficult situation with your relationships, pray and ask God for the right way to approach the situation. It might be

THE FEAR OF THE LORD IS WISDOM

a family member or a close friend or a difficult situation at work. Not everyone is a Christian, but that is exactly why you are here—to spread the Word of God and to fulfill God's true desire for you. God loves you and wishes for all to be saved and that none should perish (John 3:16-17). If you are in a difficult situation with a relationship, consider inviting that person to church or have someone come to the person's home if they agree. God has all the answers. There is nothing too difficult for God, but God will not force His will on you or anyone else.

In my case, it seems as if He did, but I really needed Him to wake me up. Maybe that's why God is using you—to wake that person up. Always allow yourself to be used for the work and glory of God, and remember to put heaven first, not earth. Our life on earth is only temporary. Think of your eternal home. Ask yourself what you can do for God and how you can help spread the Word of God. Look for ways and chances to serve God. The rewards will be greater than you can imagine. God does not only pay 100 percent, but He also gives you extra dividends.

There will be times when you will have your faith tested; you may feel weak or unable to handle the situation. You may even feel like God is not there or does not exist. That is exactly why you need to put on the whole armor of God. You can mentally put His armor on every day and at those moments of weakness, ask God for wisdom. These are the moments to get down on your knees, bow your head, and repent of your sins. Pray until you are fully filled with the Holy Spirit and you have strength again to fight the good fight. Fill yourself with God's love, His strength, and His wisdom. Do not

YOUR ARMOR

leave on empty or half tank. Don't leave until the tank is overflowing with wisdom and strength.

> O the depth of the riches both of the wisdom and knowledge of God! how unsearchable *are* his judgments, and his ways past finding out! For who hath known the mind of the Lord? or who hath been his counselor? Or who hath first given to him, and it shall be recompensed unto him again? For of him, and through him, and to him, *are* all things: to whom *be* glory for ever. Amen. (Romans 11:33-36)

Wisdom Reflections

25

REACTIONS

[Wisdom] *is* a tree of life to them that lay hold upon her:
and happy *is every one* that retaineth her.

—PROVERBS 3:18

Your reactions to upsetting situations say much about you as a person. Stop and ask God to give you wisdom when you are upset. Just take a few seconds before you say something. Consider if God's wisdom is present in this situation, or are you just reacting on your own.

Avoid saying too much or making a decision when you are upset; avoid talking if you are emotionally charged. If you are just upset and feel like screaming or yelling at the top of your lungs, stop, pray, and ask for God's help. You may need to remove yourself from the situation until you can sort it out with God. God's wisdom is greater than our wisdom. In fact, His wisdom makes our wisdom look like foolishness. God's power is greater than our weakness. God's greatness is greater than our sin. God is greater than any enemy you and I can have.[23]

REACTIONS

Consider how you treat others. Are your actions and words compassionate or are you being mean and unforgiving? Are you being abusive, emotionally or physically? Your actions also have direct reactions in your life and the lives of others. If you have consistent negative behavior towards others, over time it can affect them psychologically and you as well. Your behavior, attitude, and demeanor have lasting impressions. Be wise in what you say and how you say it. Wise is the person who measures his words. Proverbs 10:19 says that in multitude of speaking sin is not lacking. Proverbs 18:21 says that life and death are in the tongue. Be careful how much you talk. The fish is caught by opening its mouth. Words are very powerful.

When dealing with an upsetting situation focus on God, not your anger or emotions. This will allow you some space to think and reflect. Ask God to give you wisdom on how to react to the situation in a calm, cool, and collective manner.

Wisdom Reflections

26

ACT

[Wisdom] *is* a tree of life to them that lay hold upon her:
and happy *is every one* that retaineth her.

—PROVERBS 3:18

Several years ago I came up with an acronym for a security training program, but it applies to everyday life. It's called ACT (Awareness, Control, and Timing). If you apply these three principles in your life, they can have a positive impact in helping you make decisions. It's a methodical way of reacting to situations or making decisions. It helps you take into account everything that's happening at that moment and it helps you analyze if you are in complete control of all your emotions. It also helps you determine if the timing is right.

Look at each step individually and then as a whole. Try to apply them to your life. I truly believe these principles can enhance your life in and at every level. I think you might be very surprised at the results. For instance, consider its effectiveness while engaging someone in a conversation. Think to yourself, am I aware of myself and my surroundings with this person? How am I responding to them? Am I in control of my emotions and how do I feel right now? Is it the right or wrong timing to share my thoughts with this person? Maybe it's not the right place to talk and there would be a better time to share with them. This calm and collected approach could improve your life overall.

Of course nothing I create on my own is ever better than God's plan and His ways, but I believe God gave me the wisdom to apply these principles. Seek God's Word in all things and in all ways. Make sure your ideas line up with what the Word says and works for good. The Bible is the only true source of wisdom and understanding. God's ways are not our ways and His will is not our will.[24]

REMEMBER GOD

Remember now thy Creator in the days of thy youth, while the evil days come not, nor the years draw nigh, when thou shalt say, I have no pleasure in them; While the sun, or the light, or the moon, or the stars, be not darkened, nor the clouds return after the rain: In the day when the keepers of the house shall tremble, and the strong men shall bow themselves, and the grinders cease because they are few, and those that look out of the windows be darkened, And the doors shall be shut in the streets, when the sound of the grinding is low, and he shall rise up at the voice of the bird, and all

THE FEAR OF THE LORD IS WISDOM

the daughters of musick shall be brought low; Also *when* they shall be afraid of *that which is* high, and fears *shall be* in the way, and the almond tree shall flourish, and the grasshopper shall be a burden, and desire shall fail: because man goeth to his long home, and the mourners go about the streets: Or ever the silver cord be loosed, or the golden bowl be broken, or the pitcher be broken at the fountain, or the wheel broken at the cistern. Then shall the dust return to the earth as it was: and the spirit shall return unto God who gave it.

Vanity of vanities, saith the preacher; all *is* vanity. And moreover, because the preacher was wise, he still taught the people knowledge; yea, he gave good heed, and sought out, *and* set in order many proverbs. The preacher sought to find out acceptable words: and *that which was* written *was* upright, *even* words of truth. The words of the wise *are* as goads, and as nails fastened *by* the masters of assemblies, *which* are given from one shepherd. And further, by these, my son, be admonished: of making many books *there is* no end; and much study *is* a weariness of the flesh.

Let us hear the conclusion of the whole matter: Fear God, and keep his commandments: for this *is* the whole *duty* of man. For God shall bring every work into judgment, with every secret thing, whether *it be* good, or whether *it be* evil. (Ecclesiastes 12)

Wisdom Reflections

27

QUESTIONS

[Wisdom] *is* a tree of life to them that lay hold upon her:
and happy *is every one* that retaineth her.

—PROVERBS 3:18

Consider the questions below about your life and be honest. God is watching and listening; He knows your heart and He is ready to help.

Are you a good person? If not, why?

Are you a sinner?

When was the last time you said "I love you" to anybody including yourself?

When did you take time for your kids, loved ones, or a stranger?

Who was the last person you said "thank you" to?

How do you look at the homeless? How do you feel when you see them? What are your thoughts and attitudes?

THE FEAR OF THE LORD IS WISDOM

Do you think of others or only yourself and your family?

What is the most important thing in your life right now?

What makes you happy? When was the last time you were happy?

Do you love yourself?

Do you love your spouse?

Do you love your family?

How do you feel about the kind of work you do?

Are you proud of what you do for a living?

Are you proud of yourself?

Look back a year; do you see yourself going forward or backward?

What have you done with Jesus?

What have you done for Jesus?

What will your great judgment before God be like?

Will there be rewards or shame?

What do you love in life right now?

When was the last time you forgave someone—who and why?

How do you really feel about your in-laws?

How do you feel about yourself after these questions?

QUESTIONS

IDOLS

Not unto us, O LORD, not unto us, but unto thy name give glory, for thy mercy, *and* for thy truth's sake. Wherefore should the heathen say, Where *is* now their God? But our God *is* in the heavens: he hath done whatsoever he hath pleased. Their idols *are* silver and gold, the work of men's hands. They have mouths, but they speak not: eyes have they, but they see not: They have ears, but they hear not: noses have they, but they smell not: They have hands, but they handle not: feet have they, but they walk not: neither speak they through their throat. They that make them are like unto them; *so is* every one that trusteth in them.

O Israel, trust thou in the LORD: he *is* their help and their shield. O house of Aaron, trust in the LORD: he *is* their help and their shield. Ye that fear the LORD, trust in the LORD: he *is* their help and their shield. The LORD hath been mindful of us: he will bless *us*; he will bless the house of Israel; he will bless the house of Aaron. He will bless them that fear the LORD, *both* small and great. The LORD shall increase you more and more, you and your children. Ye *are* blessed of the LORD which made heaven and earth. The heaven, *even* the heavens, *are* the LORD'S: but the earth hath he given to the children of men. The dead

THE FEAR OF THE LORD IS WISDOM

praise not the LORD, neither any that go down into silence. But we will bless the LORD from this time forth and for evermore. Praise the LORD. (Psalms 115)

Wisdom Reflections

28

COMMITTED

[Wisdom] is a tree of life to them that lay hold upon her:
and happy is every one that retaineth her.

—PROVERBS 3:18

Consider the power of wisdom; its abilities are endless. Wisdom does not come from man but from above. Understanding does not come from man but from above. There is no real power but God's power. You must believe that in your heart, know it your heart, and understand it with your soul, for there is only power in God. When you are in times of need, lacking faith, or in pain, remember God's wisdom is greater than your problem. God's power is greater than your weakness.

Please understand that you must commit and submit yourself to God. Be like a lamb, blameless and seeking only the true shepherd which is Christ. God knows His sheep and He knows the goats and separates them. Live a life according to God's laws and ways. Do not involve yourself with the world or you will end up being a part of them. Seek God's face in every situation and know that God is there.

THE FEAR OF THE LORD IS WISDOM

He knows when you are in times of distress or when you feel like a coward. Take refuge in God's arms. Tell God you are not strong enough without Him. Admit you are a sinner and that you need help. Admit you want to change but you can't do it on your own. Put your faith in Christ. Ask Christ to come to your life. Ask the Holy Spirit to fill you with God's love and grace. When you sin, immediately ask for forgiveness in Jesus' name.

Do not forget about God in the good times. Seek Him in moments of despair or great pain and anguish, but remember God at all times and in all things. When you feel that you need more wisdom, simply ask God and He will give it to you generously. Just be honest and explain to God that you need His help. You need His love, His direction, and His guidance. Humble yourself before God.

If you have accepted Christ, remember that the old self is dead. You are a new creature. You were purchased at a great price by the very blood and body of Jesus Christ. It's a gift and He saw you as valuable enough to give His son for you. Commit to Him.

GOD TAKES US BACK

And he said, A certain man had two sons: And the younger of them said to *his* father, Father, give me the portion of goods that falleth *to me*. And he divided unto them *his* living. And not many days after the younger son gathered all together, and took his journey into a far country, and there wasted his substance with riotous living. And when he had spent all, there arose a mighty famine in that land; and he began to be in want. And he went and joined himself to a citizen of that country; and he sent him into his fields to feed swine. And he would fain have filled his belly with the husks that the swine did eat: and no man gave unto him.

And when he came to himself, he said, How many hired servants of my father's have bread enough and to spare, and I perish with hunger! I will arise and go to my father, and will say unto him, Father, I have sinned against heaven, and before thee, And am no more worthy to be called thy son: make me as one of thy hired servants. And he arose, and came to his father. But when he was yet a great way off, his father saw him, and had compassion, and ran, and fell on his neck, and kissed him. And the son said unto him, Father, I have sinned against heaven, and in thy sight, and am no more worthy to be called thy son. But the father said to his servants, Bring forth the best robe, and put *it* on him; and put a ring on his hand, and shoes on *his* feet: And bring hither the fatted calf, and kill *it*; and let us eat, and be merry: For this my son was dead, and is alive again; he was lost, and is found. And they began to be merry.

Now his elder son was in the field: and as he came and drew nigh to the house, he heard music and dancing. And he called one of the servants, and asked what these things meant. And he said unto him, Thy brother is come; and thy father hath killed the fatted calf, because he hath received him safe and sound. And he was angry, and would not go in: therefore came his father out, and intreated him. And he answering said to *his* father, Lo, these many years do I serve thee, neither transgressed I at any time thy commandment: and yet thou never gavest me a kid, that I might make merry with my friends: But as soon as this thy son was come, which hath devoured thy living with harlots, thou hast killed for him the fatted calf. And he said unto him, Son, thou art ever with me, and all that I have is thine. It was meet that we should make merry, and be glad: for this thy brother was dead, and is alive again; and was lost, and is found. (Luke 15:11-32)

Wisdom Reflections

29

MASKS

[Wisdom] *is* a tree of life to them that lay hold upon her:
and happy *is every one* that retaineth her.

—PROVERBS 3:18

We often attempt to change others, but you must first change yourself. It took me a lot of tears and pain, but I finally learned that I can only change me. God must change others. Learn who you are. Learn to identify your strengths and weakness. Learn to build on your strength and turn even your weakness into strength. When we look at our weakness, we are seeing what we can learn from them if looked at in the right way. Listen, look, and identify why you have those weakness. Are you covering something by wearing a mask? Believe it or not, we wear masks for different events and places. We all wear masks for many reasons, mainly to fit in and blend or to be noticed.

Do you wear a mask?

Do you wear many?

What is your mask for?

THE FEAR OF THE LORD IS WISDOM

Masks seem to be useful for many different things, but they are not good because they are all lies. I understand that you cannot be *yourself* all the time because of work or environments that may be inappropriate, but I am asking you to look at yourself when you wear your mask and see how you behave. How different are you with yourself and others? How is your facial expression and body language? What kind of clothes and posture do you wear? How do you conduct yourself? Wouldn't it be nice to love yourself when you are yourself? Think about that for a moment. How does wearing the mask make you feel? What do you gain and lose by wearing a mask? Which is your favorite mask and why? Which mask do you wear the most and why? This is very personal and private but you must be willing to look and take off your mask and see yourself. God sees behind your masks.

CONSIDER WISDOM'S WAY

The power of wisdom requires one to search oneself in all ways of the heart, mind, and soul. One must get used to looking at and examining oneself in ways that reflects the good, the bad, and the ugly. Everyone has attitudes, habits, and behaviors that we do not like. That is why we examine our choices and reflect on them, good and bad. There have been many times that I have looked back at my life and asked, "Why?" The question itself is very powerful. Why did I react or fail to react in a manner or fashion that would have been suitable or appropriate? One does not even realize at

MASKS

times the magnitude or effect their actions or lack of making decisions that will have an impact on their lives and others. Your actions and failures to react will create your world either for good or bad. Remember, with God there is always hope.

Wisdom Reflections

30

YOURSELF

[Wisdom] *is* a tree of life to them that lay hold upon her:
and happy *is every one* that retaineth her.

—PROVERBS 3:18

Really look at yourself and be honest. Do you like what you see, hear, and feel? If not, pray with me right now and say, "Lord Jesus, please change me from the inside out. I want to change to be more like You, My Lord Jesus, amen. Help me to love myself. I want to change as a person; I want to be a better Christian, a better human being, a better (father/mother, son/daughter, husband/wife, or friend.)"

Tell God how much you really want to change. God can do anything. Consider the Apostle Paul. He wrote eleven chapters of the Bible, but prior to his conversion to Christianity he was killing Christians! God had a plan for him even though he was vehemently opposed to the initial movement of Christianity. He took God's beautiful offer. It's being offered to you right now. Change and become a new you—the one that God intended you to be through

YOURSELF

Christ our Lord and Savior. There are things about me that I actually hate, but God's love covers them all. He heals my brokenness, but I still want Him to change me, to help me grow. Let God know you want to change and become a true child of God.

Wisdom Reflections

3 1

ENDORSEMENT

[Wisdom] *is* a tree of life to them that lay hold upon her:
and happy *is every one* that retaineth her.

—PROVERBS 3:18

Reflect on the activities of your life. The things that you do on a regular basis are things that you endorse. You give those things your blessing. Consider if you want to be part of those activities. Much can be said about who stays and goes at the work site or the party. Do you want to be part of those things? The situations of your life affect you and those in your circle of influence—directly and indirectly. Are you pleased with your activities? You might be surprised at the answer. I know I have been surprised at my own.

Wisdom is the key to everything and wisdom only comes from God. Ask God about difficult decisions, choices, or things you aren't sure of. He hears you and will respond in ways that will amaze you. What I love is that the answer is for you alone. God is very personal with us. He is an intimate, loving, and caring God. Remember, God cannot change; He is love. Pray about your decisions and keep

ENDORSEMENT

them before the Father. Sometimes God's silence is the answer and sometimes He simply leads you by the peace in your heart. Seek His wisdom, His understanding, and His counsel. Ask God if He is pleased with your participation in the events of your life. Listen for His peace and confirmation before you endorse anything with your presence.

CONSIDER WISDOM'S WAY

Put on the whole armor of God and fight the good fight of faith. Read Jeremiah 29:13. Seek God and you will find him. It's a narrow gate to heaven, but wide is the gate to hell. Jesus the price for you to go to heaven, but when we sin willfully and without remorse, we do not respect God's decision and the price he paid for us. For God so loved the world that Christ saved us while we were sinners (John 3:16). Please remember we are still sinners.

I think every day of my prize in heaven. Each will be rewarded based on your work for Christ. Salvation is a gift, but rewards are earned through Christ. What will you do for Jesus? God is our reward. I have a reward and crown that I fight for every day.

Wisdom Reflections

3 2

WORK

[Wisdom] *is* a tree of life to them that lay hold upon her:
and happy *is every one* that retaineth her.

—PROVERBS 3:18

There are moments I say, "I can't do this." In my work as a police officer, for example, I sometimes feel overwhelmed. We have had a lot of changes in our unit and I have had to grow personally. Your work affects you in every aspect of your life. Work consumes so much of your time that it really is a great portion of how you live and how you make a living. God provides always, and ultimately, it's all his.

Consider how you spend your forty-plus hours a week. Write your thoughts and attitudes toward your work down. I am now learning through Christ (the very wisdom of God) how much this really impacts us. Evaluate your facial expression, your eyes, your breathing, and your thoughts about your career. Is it what you want and where you want to be? Do you believe that God called you to do

WORK

what you are doing? You take it all home and bring it back the next day. Does it bring glory to God?

Your work makes a difference in your life—what you are paid, the satisfaction it brings—but what are you willing to lose or gain because of it? Jesus said, "What does it profit if a man if he gains the whole world and loses his soul?"[25] I think about the garden of Gethsemane. I was there in Jerusalem. Jesus made the choice that no one else could ever make or would. Jesus chose you.

How many birthdays, parties, church attendances, holidays, or family get-togethers have you missed? There is always a price. Is it worth it? Did He call you to it? What did you gain and what did you lose? If you want to work and you should work, just make sure you are working toward your reward in heaven.

Wisdom Reflections

33

PEOPLE

> [Wisdom] *is* a tree of life to them that lay hold upon her:
> and happy *is every one* that retaineth her.
>
> —PROVERBS 3:18

There are so many things unseen that we do not even consider in our life. We don't know what other people are going through. Just because you and I don't understand or care to understand, that does not mean it's not important. We typically justify everything to our standard of how things should be done or the way we view life. Look beyond what we see in our natural man and look at the true source. Many times we only react to what we can see. That's the problem. We don't see beyond because we only react to what is obvious. Take your time before you react to others. It makes a world of difference. How you choose to react to people has a lifetime of consequences.

Look at all the people in prison. Some of them are good people that made some bad choices. Many of them belong there, but some just reacted to situation and did stop and think about their choice. How many times did you just react and regret the outcome? You

PEOPLE

may want to write down the five best choices or decisions and five worst. It would be a good exercise to write down your life story from start to finish. Write about the days and moments that changed you. Reflect on everything that was going in your life at that time and your pattern of thinking. What could you have done differently and why?

This exercise is not to hurt you in any way. Actually it should allow you to see yourself in totally different light. Reflect on who you were you talking to that day. For example, let's say you were arguing over the phone with someone or maybe you were face-to-face. After they were done with all the yelling, did they eventually calm down? Reflect on how many conversations or problems have gotten out of control because of your lack of self-control or self-awareness. Monitor your behavior. Look at yourself from the outside and then look at yourself from the inside out. What do you see, and how do you feel about the situation, and could you have handled yourself differently? Learn from your mistakes. Learn to govern yourself.

Reflect on yourself and your actions. Good or bad? Are you supportive or non-supportive? Are you helpful or hurtful? When your kids fight among themselves, whose side do you take? Evaluate that process. Is it because he or she is your favorite, or is it because the other child is more disobedient? Is it because you are getting back to your spouse through your kids? Is God pleased with your behavior?

True understanding comes from God, and only God knows what true understanding is. Take time out of your day, not only to

THE FEAR OF THE LORD IS WISDOM

pray but to look back at the choices and decisions you have made that day. Are they good or bad? What kind of long or short term effects do they have on the people you love and the people God loves?

Wisdom Reflections

3 4

DO GOOD

[Wisdom] *is* a tree of life to them that lay hold upon her: and happy *is every one* that retaineth her.

—PROVERBS 3:18

Jesus, seeing the multitudes, went up into a mountain; and when he was set, his disciples came unto him, and he opened his mouth and taught them, saying,

Blessed *are* the poor in spirit: for theirs is the kingdom of heaven. Blessed *are* they that mourn: for they shall be comforted. Blessed *are* the meek: for they shall inherit the earth. Blessed *are* they which do hunger and thirst after righteousness: for they shall be filled. Blessed *are* the merciful: for they shall obtain mercy. Blessed *are* the pure in heart: for they shall see God. Blessed *are* the peacemakers: for they shall be called the children of God. Blessed *are* they which are persecuted for righteousness' sake: for theirs is the kingdom of heaven. Blessed are ye, when *men* shall revile you, and persecute *you*, and shall say all manner of evil against you falsely, for my sake. Rejoice, and be exceeding

THE FEAR OF THE LORD IS WISDOM

glad: for great *is* your reward in heaven: for so persecuted they the prophets which were before you. (Matthew 5:1-12)

Look at the rich and the poor. Does either care for the other? Each seeks their own way. If all gave, we would not be where we are in life. I am not saying there are no people out there trying to do good; I know that there are, *but how many?*

Conversations with God
WHY IS THERE SUFFERING?

ACCUSER: Well, GOD, You made us and we are all Your creation; are we not?

GOD: Yes, but I did not create sin.

ACCUSER: But, God, don't You know everything?

GOD: Yes, but you still have free *will.*

ACCUSER: How can you watch all of this suffering?

GOD: I gave you Jesus, the Christ, my only Son. *I watched Him suffer for you and I suffered with Him, for We are one. I watched myself suffer.*

ACCUSER: Why allow all this pain in the world?

GOD: Why do you think it's okay and acceptable to sin and break my laws and my commandments? Why is murder, theft,

DO GOOD

fornication, pornography, *fraud,* and all other forms of sin allowed and tolerated?

ACCUSER: Okay, but what about all the suffering?

GOD: What about all the sin?

ACCUSER: Why do you not stop suffering?

GOD: Why don't you stop *sinning?* Pain and suffering are results of sin.

ACCUSER: Not everyone is bad.

GOD: All have *gone astray.* There is none that is righteous before Me, not one. *No one seeks Me* or knows My heart. My ways are not your ways. My Word says of Jesus: Surely He hath borne our griefs, and carried our sorrows: yet we did esteem Him stricken, smitten of God, and afflicted. But He *was* wounded for our transgressions; *He was* bruised for our iniquities: the chastisement of our peace *was* upon *H*im; and with His stripes we are healed. All we like sheep have gone astray; we have turned every one to his own way; and the LORD hath laid on Him the iniquity of us all (Isaiah 53:4-6).

ACCUSER: Yes, but not all people are bad.

GOD: No one is righteous but I, for my only Son came to save that which was lost.

ACCUSER: What's changed since Christ?

GOD: You now have access to me, right here, right now. You are saved through His blood; only through Jesus is there salvation—only through Jesus the Christ, the only begotten son of the living God.

THE FEAR OF THE LORD IS WISDOM

ACCUSER: What do You mean?

GOD: We are communicating; aren't we, *right now?*

ACCUSER: What about the other religions? Are they all bad or wrong?

GOD: Only through My Son Jesus, My Lamb, do You have access to Me. For Jesus is the way, the truth, the life. I paid for your salvation. Who else has redeemed all of you? I hung on the cross by choice for you because I *Am love.* Only through Jesus Christ can you know Me and be accepted. Only by Jesus will I know you as Mine. Many are called but few are chosen. Many think they are My flock but are not! I was raised from the dead. I laid down My life and took it back. Who else has done that?

ACCUSER: Okay, but what about *good work?*

GOD: Who is good among you? Who is righteous? Who has never sinned?

ACCUSER: Okay, You got me.

GOD: I love all of you. Seek My face, My heart, My spirit, My love. I Am with you always *even until end.* For those who are Mine, there is no death. There is no dying.

ACCUSER: Where are You, God?

GOD: I was on the cross and when that person next to Me was dying, I did not call him a thief but a person. That's how I look at My children. There were two of them; both could have been saved. One died in his sin. The other did not and was saved by faith in Me.

DO GOOD

You often ask where I Am. I was right there dying for you and the whole world. I gave you another chance; life or death, it's your choice. I died so you could have true freedom to choose life or death.

You often put Me in a small box. If heaven cannot contain Me, how can your box contain Me? How small would I be if I fit in your box? What kind of God fits in a box? Only false idols and worthless artifacts. Remember, it's your box not Mine. I Am bigger than your box.

What box are you in? Ask Me and we will get you out together. My power is bigger than the biggest of your problems, boxes, or issues. I Am bigger than your sin. I have overcome sin to bring you life through Me.

ACCUSER: Who is wise?

GOD: Only I, for I give wisdom because I am wisdom and understanding.

Those who seek Me, find Me; and those who talk and pray humbly to Me, I hear. Their prayers, their words pierce through the very clouds straight into heaven. I love those who love Me *and those who don't*.

ACCUSER: God?

GOD: Yes.

ACCUSER: How can I experience Your love?

GOD: Accept My free gift of salvation, *accept Me, repent,* and accept Jesus as your Lord and Savior. Turn your heart, your mind, and your ways from sins. I will accept you and no wise cast you away.

THE FEAR OF THE LORD IS WISDOM

ACCUSER: (Crying) Jesus, I accept You as my Lord and Savior; and ask to be forgiven of my sins. I repent. Amen.

Ask yourself right now, this moment, have you accepted Christ in your life? Are you saved? Accept God's offer right now. Do not wait; there is nothing to lose, but there is everything to gain. Accept Jesus Christ right now.

Say this prayer sincerely:

"Dear God, I pray in Jesus' name, Your lamb, the Christ, who came to save the world. I repent of my ways and ask Jesus into my life as my Lord and savior. I know I am a sinner, and I want to be saved. Please, Jesus, accept me and welcome me into the family of heaven. I ask and pray that the holy blood of Jesus Christ, the son and Lamb of God, wash away all of my sins, and make me a child of the living God. Holy Spirit, please grant wisdom, understanding, and counsel to me. May my life be counted worthy and acceptable to You, my Lord and savior Jesus. Amen."

God bless you.

Above all, fear God and obey his commandments.
Jesus the way, the truth and the life.
The power of wisdom.
The path of understanding.
The crown of wisdom.

DO GOOD

Wisdom from the Scriptures
JESUS' PRAYER HIS DISCIPLES AND FOR YOU

"I have manifested Your name to the men whom You have given Me out of the world. They were Yours, You gave them to Me, and they have kept Your word. Now they have known that all things which You have given Me are from You. For I have given to them the words which You have given Me; and they have received *them*, and have known surely that I came forth from You; and they have believed that You sent Me.

"I pray for them. I do not pray for the world but for those whom You have given Me, for they are Yours. And all Mine are Yours, and Yours are Mine, and I am glorified in them. Now I am no longer in the world, but these are in the world, and I come to You. Holy Father, keep through Your name those whom You have given Me, that they may be one as We *are*. While I was with them in the world, I kept them in Your name. Those whom You gave Me I have kept; and none of them is lost except the son of perdition, that the Scripture might be fulfilled. But now I come to You, and these things I speak in the world, that they may have My joy fulfilled in themselves. I have given them Your word; and the world has hated them because they are not of the world, just as I am not of the world. I do not pray that You should take them out of the world, but that You should keep them

THE FEAR OF THE LORD IS WISDOM

from the evil one. They are not of the world, just as I am not of the world. Sanctify them by Your truth. Your word is truth. As You sent Me into the world, I also have sent them into the world. And for their sakes I sanctify Myself, that they also may be sanctified by the truth.

"I do not pray for these alone, but also for those who will believe in Me through their word; that they all may be one, as You, Father, *are* in Me, and I in You; that they also may be one in Us, that the world may believe that You sent Me. And the glory which You gave Me I have given them, that they may be one just as We are one: I in them, and You in Me; that they may be made perfect in one, and that the world may know that You have sent Me, and have loved them as You have loved Me.

"Father, I desire that they also whom You gave Me may be with Me where I am, that they may behold My glory which You have given Me; for You loved Me before the foundation of the world. O righteous Father! The world has not known You, but I have known You; and these have known that You sent Me. And I have declared to them Your name, and will declare *it,* that the love with which You loved Me may be in them, and I in them." (John 17:6-26 NKJV)

CONCLUSION

We started this journey together and the quest for wisdom is a journey we will continue for the rest of our lives. God has so much for you and me. We will only continue to grow in Christ.

Please consider the following questions before you end this book.

What does wisdom mean to you?

What is godly wisdom versus worldly wisdom?

What is the difference between other religions and Christianity?

What does Jesus Christ offer you that no one can?

Who loves like God?

Who is like God?

How do you feel about God?

What is understanding?

How do you love others?

How do you understand life?

How will you react to people, situations, and events now?

Where are you in life and how did you get there?

Where are you going now?

What separates you from God right now?

THE FEAR OF THE LORD IS WISDOM

Do your sins or your habits separate you from God?

Is it your lifestyle your way of thinking, or your way of living?

Is there a particular hobby or way of living you can't give up, or worse, won't give up?

Continue to evaluate your life and your actions. Lay everything before Him. Continue to seek His wisdom in every area of your life.

God bless you on your quest.

ACKNOWLEDGEMENT

I would first like to thank and praise God through his son Jesus Christ. I would like thank and Praise the Holy Spirit without whom this could have not been done. I would like to further thank the Yorkshire Publishing Group starting with Todd Rutherford who had the vision, honesty, and Godly value to ensure my book was done right. I would like to thank the whole Yorkshire Publishing Family for taking their time and for everything that they have done.

I would like to thank Amanda Pilgrim, Kevin, and Brian and the whole Yorkshire Publishing Family. Thank you for your values, integrity, and above **ALL FEAR of God.**

May God be praised and pleased with us, may our work be considered worthy before our Lord and Savior. May all of us receive a crown by our Savior. Most of all may we be found pleasing in God eyes.

> May wisdom be in our heart, soul, and mind,
> May understanding breath in us knowledge and insight,
> May God's Holy Spirit be in us at all times.

To all who have not accepted Jesus as their Lord and Savior, please make the most important choice in your life. Say this prayer with me, it has EnTERNAL EFFECTS:

THE FEAR OF THE LORD IS WISDOM

Dear God,

I come to you as a sinner, I accept your son Jesus Christ as my Lord and Savior.

I accept what he and only he could do at the cross for us. Thank you God for sending Jesus to die in my place. I now wish to be a child of God through Jesus Christ.

May I fear, love, and obey your laws.

Amen

Thank you. MAY GOD RICHLY BLESS YOU NOW AND THE LIFE AFTER.

NOTES

1. Exodus 14
2. Genesis 15-17
3. Matthew 19:26
4. Matthew 22:39
5. Luke 22:42
6. 2 Corinthians 5:21
7. Matthew 27:16-26
8. John 8:7
9. Luke 1:37
10. James 4:6
11. Matthew 22:39
12. 1 Peter 4:8
13. John 10:11
14. John 14:15
15. 2 Corinthians 5:17
16. Habakkuk 2:2
17. 1 Corinthians 10:13
18. Ephesians 6:10-18
19. 2 Corinthians 12:9
20. Galatians 5:17
21. 2 Timothy 1:7
22. Psalm 27:8
23. Romans 8:31
24. Isaiah 55:8
25. Matthew 16:26

PRAY AND THINK ABOUT PSALM 119 AND 128

Psalm 119 (New King James Version)

Psalm 119

ALEPH

1 Blessed *are* the undefiled in the way,
   Who walk in the law of the LORD!

2 Blessed *are* those who keep His testimonies,
   Who seek Him with the whole heart!

3 They also do no iniquity;
   They walk in His ways.

4 You have commanded *us*
   To keep Your precepts diligently.

5 Oh, that my ways were directed
   To keep Your statutes!

6 Then I would not be ashamed,
   When I look into all Your commandments.

7 I will praise You with uprightness of heart,
   When I learn Your righteous judgments.

8 I will keep Your statutes;
   Oh, do not forsake me utterly!

BETH

9 How can a young man cleanse his way?
   By taking heed according to Your word.

10 With my whole heart I have sought You;
    Oh, let me not wander from Your commandments!

PRAY AND THINK ABOUT PSALM 119 AND 128

11 Your word I have hidden in my heart,
    That I might not sin against You.

12 Blessed *are* You, O LORD!
    Teach me Your statutes.

13 With my lips I have declared
    All the judgments of Your mouth.

14 I have rejoiced in the way of Your testimonies,
    As *much as* in all riches.

15 I will meditate on Your precepts,
    And contemplate Your ways.

16 I will delight myself in Your statutes;
    I will not forget Your word.

GIMEL

17 Deal bountifully with Your servant,
    That I may live and keep Your word.

18 Open my eyes, that I may see
    Wondrous things from Your law.

19 I *am* a stranger in the earth;
    Do not hide Your commandments from me.

20 My soul breaks with longing
    For Your judgments at all times.

21 You rebuke the proud—the cursed,
    Who stray from Your commandments.

22 Remove from me reproach and contempt,
    For I have kept Your testimonies.

23 Princes also sit *and* speak against me,
    But Your servant meditates on Your statutes.

24 Your testimonies also *are* my delight
    And my counselors.

THE FEAR OF THE LORD IS WISDOM

DALETH

25 My soul clings to the dust;
  Revive me according to Your word.

26 I have declared my ways, and You answered me;
  Teach me Your statutes.

27 Make me understand the way of Your precepts;
  So shall I meditate on Your wonderful works.

28 My soul melts from heaviness;
  Strengthen me according to Your word.

29 Remove from me the way of lying,
  And grant me Your law graciously.

30 I have chosen the way of truth;
  Your judgments I have laid *before me.*

31 I cling to Your testimonies;
  O LORD, do not put me to shame!

32 I will run the course of Your commandments,
  For You shall enlarge my heart.

HE

33 Teach me, O LORD, the way of Your statutes,
  And I shall keep it *to* the end.

34 Give me understanding, and I shall keep Your law;
  Indeed, I shall observe it with *my* whole heart.

35 Make me walk in the path of Your commandments,
  For I delight in it.

36 Incline my heart to Your testimonies,
  And not to covetousness.

37 Turn away my eyes from looking at worthless things,
  And revive me in Your way.[a]

PRAY AND THINK ABOUT PSALM 119 AND 128

38 Establish Your word to Your servant,
   Who *is devoted* to fearing You.
39 Turn away my reproach which I dread,
   For Your judgments *are* good.
40 Behold, I long for Your precepts;
   Revive me in Your righteousness.

WAW

41 Let Your mercies come also to me, O LORD—
   Your salvation according to Your word.
42 So shall I have an answer for him who reproaches me,
   For I trust in Your word.
43 And take not the word of truth utterly out of my mouth,
   For I have hoped in Your ordinances.
44 So shall I keep Your law continually,
   Forever and ever.
45 And I will walk at liberty,
   For I seek Your precepts.
46 I will speak of Your testimonies also before kings,
   And will not be ashamed.
47 And I will delight myself in Your commandments,
   Which I love.
48 My hands also I will lift up to Your commandments,
   Which I love,
   And I will meditate on Your statutes.

ZAYIN

49 Remember the word to Your servant,
   Upon which You have caused me to hope.

THE FEAR OF THE LORD IS WISDOM

50 This *is* my comfort in my affliction,
   For Your word has given me life.
51 The proud have me in great derision,
   Yet I do not turn aside from Your law.
52 I remembered Your judgments of old, O LORD,
   And have comforted myself.
53 Indignation has taken hold of me
   Because of the wicked, who forsake Your law.
   54 Your statutes have been my songs
   In the house of my pilgrimage.
55 I remember Your name in the night, O LORD,
   And I keep Your law.
56 This has become mine,
   Because I kept Your precepts.

HETH

57 *You are* my portion, O LORD;
   I have said that I would keep Your words.
58 I entreated Your favor with *my* whole heart;
   Be merciful to me according to Your word.
59 I thought about my ways,
   And turned my feet to Your testimonies.
60 I made haste, and did not delay
   To keep Your commandments.
61 The cords of the wicked have bound me,
   But I have not forgotten Your law.
62 At midnight I will rise to give thanks to You,
   Because of Your righteous judgments.
63 I *am* a companion of all who fear You,
   And of those who keep Your precepts.

64 The earth, O LORD, is full of Your mercy;
   Teach me Your statutes.

TETH

65 You have dealt well with Your servant,
   O LORD, according to Your word.

66 Teach me good judgment and knowledge,
   For I believe Your commandments.

67 Before I was afflicted I went astray,
   But now I keep Your word.

68 You *are* good, and do good;
   Teach me Your statutes.

69 The proud have forged a lie against me,
   But I will keep Your precepts with *my* whole heart.

70 Their heart is as fat as grease,
   But I delight in Your law.

71 *It is* good for me that I have been afflicted,
   That I may learn Your statutes.

72 The law of Your mouth *is* better to me
   Than thousands of *coins of* gold and silver.

YOD

73 Your hands have made me and fashioned me;
   Give me understanding, that I may learn Your commandments.

74 Those who fear You will be glad when they see me,
   Because I have hoped in Your word.

75 I know, O LORD, that Your judgments *are* right,
   And *that* in faithfulness You have afflicted me.

THE FEAR OF THE LORD IS WISDOM

76 Let, I pray, Your merciful kindness be for my comfort,
  According to Your word to Your servant.

77 Let Your tender mercies come to me, that I may live;
  For Your law *is* my delight.

78 Let the proud be ashamed,
  For they treated me wrongfully with falsehood;
  But I will meditate on Your precepts.

79 Let those who fear You turn to me,
  Those who know Your testimonies.

80 Let my heart be blameless regarding Your statutes,
  That I may not be ashamed.

KAPH

81 My soul faints for Your salvation,
  But I hope in Your word.

82 My eyes fail *from searching* Your word,
  Saying, "When will You comfort me?"

83 For I have become like a wineskin in smoke,
  Yet I do not forget Your statutes.

84 How many *are* the days of Your servant?
  When will You execute judgment on those who persecute me?

85 The proud have dug pits for me,
  Which *is* not according to Your law.

86 All Your commandments *are* faithful;
  They persecute me wrongfully;
  Help me!

87 They almost made an end of me on earth,
  But I did not forsake Your precepts.

88 Revive me according to Your lovingkindness,
   So that I may keep the testimony of Your mouth.

LAMED

89 Forever, O LORD,
   Your word is settled in heaven.

90 Your faithfulness *endures* to all generations;
   You established the earth, and it abides.

91 They continue this day according to Your ordinances,
   For all *are* Your servants.

92 Unless Your law *had been* my delight,
   I would then have perished in my affliction.

93 I will never forget Your precepts,
   For by them You have given me life.

94 I *am* Yours, save me;
   For I have sought Your precepts.

95 The wicked wait for me to destroy me,
   But I will consider Your testimonies.

96 I have seen the consummation of all perfection,
   But Your commandment *is* exceedingly broad.

MEM

97 Oh, how I love Your law!
   It *is* my meditation all the day.

98 You, through Your commandments, make me wiser than my enemies;
   For they *are* ever with me.

99 I have more understanding than all my teachers,
   For Your testimonies *are* my meditation.

THE FEAR OF THE LORD IS WISDOM

100 I understand more than the ancients,
   Because I keep Your precepts.

101 I have restrained my feet from every evil way,
   That I may keep Your word.

102 I have not departed from Your judgments,
   For You Yourself have taught me.

103 How sweet are Your words to my taste,
   Sweeter than honey to my mouth!

104 Through Your precepts I get understanding;
   Therefore I hate every false way.

NUN

105 Your word *is* a lamp to my feet
   And a light to my path.

106 I have sworn and confirmed
   That I will keep Your righteous judgments.

107 I am afflicted very much;
   Revive me, O LORD, according to Your word.

108 Accept, I pray, the freewill offerings of my mouth, O LORD,
   And teach me Your judgments.

109 My life *is* continually in my hand,
   Yet I do not forget Your law.

110 The wicked have laid a snare for me,
   Yet I have not strayed from Your precepts.

111 Your testimonies I have taken as a heritage forever,
   For they *are* the rejoicing of my heart.

112 I have inclined my heart to perform Your statutes
   Forever, to the very end.

PRAY AND THINK ABOUT PSALM 119 AND 128

SAMEK

113 I hate the double-minded,
    But I love Your law.

114 You *are* my hiding place and my shield;
    I hope in Your word.

115 Depart from me, you evildoers,
    For I will keep the commandments of my God!

116 Uphold me according to Your word, that I may live;
    And do not let me be ashamed of my hope.

117 Hold me up, and I shall be safe,
    And I shall observe Your statutes continually.

118 You reject all those who stray from Your statutes,
    For their deceit *is* falsehood.

119 You put away all the wicked of the earth *like* dross;
    Therefore I love Your testimonies.

120 My flesh trembles for fear of You,
    And I am afraid of Your judgments.

AYIN

121 I have done justice and righteousness;
    Do not leave me to my oppressors.

122 Be surety for Your servant for good;
    Do not let the proud oppress me.

123 My eyes fail *from seeking* Your salvation
    And Your righteous word.

124 Deal with Your servant according to Your mercy,
    And teach me Your statutes.

125 I *am* Your servant;
    Give me understanding,
    That I may know Your testimonies.

THE FEAR OF THE LORD IS WISDOM

126 *It is* time for *You* to act, O LORD,
   For they have regarded Your law as void.
127 Therefore I love Your commandments
   More than gold, yes, than fine gold!
128 Therefore all *Your* precepts *concerning* all *things*
   I consider *to be* right;
   I hate every false way.

PE

129 Your testimonies are wonderful;
   Therefore my soul keeps them.
130 The entrance of Your words gives light;
   It gives understanding to the simple.
131 I opened my mouth and panted,
   For I longed for Your commandments.
132 Look upon me and be merciful to me,
   As Your custom *is* toward those who love Your name.
133 Direct my steps by Your word,
   And let no iniquity have dominion over me.
134 Redeem me from the oppression of man,
   That I may keep Your precepts.
135 Make Your face shine upon Your servant,
   And teach me Your statutes.
136 Rivers of water run down from my eyes,
   Because *men* do not keep Your law.

TSADDE

137 Righteous *are* You, O LORD,
   And upright *are* Your judgments.

PRAY AND THINK ABOUT PSALM 119 AND 128

138 Your testimonies, *which* You have commanded,
   Are righteous and very faithful.

139 My zeal has consumed me,
   Because my enemies have forgotten Your words.

140 Your word *is* very pure;
   Therefore Your servant loves it.

141 I *am* small and despised,
   Yet I do not forget Your precepts.

142 Your righteousness *is* an everlasting righteousness,
   And Your law *is* truth.

143 Trouble and anguish have overtaken me,
   Yet Your commandments *are* my delights.

144 The righteousness of Your testimonies *is* everlasting;
   Give me understanding, and I shall live.

QOPH

145 I cry out with *my* whole heart;
   Hear me, O LORD!
   I will keep Your statutes.

146 I cry out to You;
   Save me, and I will keep Your testimonies.

147 I rise before the dawning of the morning,
   And cry for help;
   I hope in Your word.

148 My eyes are awake through the *night* watches,
   That I may meditate on Your word.

149 Hear my voice according to Your lovingkindness;
   O LORD, revive me according to Your justice.

150 They draw near who follow after wickedness;
   They are far from Your law.

THE FEAR OF THE LORD IS WISDOM

151 You *are* near, O LORD,
    And all Your commandments *are* truth.

152 Concerning Your testimonies,
    I have known of old that You have founded them forever.

RESH

153 Consider my affliction and deliver me,
    For I do not forget Your law.

154 Plead my cause and redeem me;
    Revive me according to Your word.

155 Salvation *is* far from the wicked,
    For they do not seek Your statutes.

156 Great *are* Your tender mercies, O LORD;
    Revive me according to Your judgments.

157 Many *are* my persecutors and my enemies,
    Yet I do not turn from Your testimonies.

158 I see the treacherous, and am disgusted,
    Because they do not keep Your word.

159 Consider how I love Your precepts;
    Revive me, O LORD, according to Your lovingkindness.

160 The entirety of Your word *is* truth,
    And every one of Your righteous judgments *endures* forever.

SHIN

161 Princes persecute me without a cause,
    But my heart stands in awe of Your word.

162 I rejoice at Your word
    As one who finds great treasure.

163 I hate and abhor lying,
    But I love Your law.

PRAY AND THINK ABOUT PSALM 119 AND 128

164 Seven times a day I praise You,
   Because of Your righteous judgments.

165 Great peace have those who love Your law,
   And nothing causes them to stumble.

166 LORD, I hope for Your salvation,
   And I do Your commandments.

167 My soul keeps Your testimonies,
   And I love them exceedingly.

168 I keep Your precepts and Your testimonies,
   For all my ways *are* before You.

TAU

169 Let my cry come before You, O LORD;
   Give me understanding according to Your word.

170 Let my supplication come before You;
   Deliver me according to Your word.

171 My lips shall utter praise,
   For You teach me Your statutes.

172 My tongue shall speak of Your word,
   For all Your commandments *are* righteousness.

173 Let Your hand become my help,
   For I have chosen Your precepts.

174 I long for Your salvation, O LORD,
   And Your law *is* my delight.

175 Let my soul live, and it shall praise You;
   And let Your judgments help me.

176 I have gone astray like a lost sheep;
   Seek Your servant,
   For I do not forget Your commandments

THE FEAR OF THE LORD IS WISDOM

Psalm 128(New King James Version)

Psalm 128

A Song of Ascents.

1 Blessed *is* every one who fears the LORD,
    Who walks in His ways.

2 When you eat the labor of your hands,
    You *shall be* happy, and *it shall be* well with you.

3 Your wife *shall be* like a fruitful vine
    In the very heart of your house,
    Your children like olive plants
    All around your table.

4 Behold, thus shall the man be blessed
    Who fears the LORD.

5 The LORD bless you out of Zion,
    And may you see the good of Jerusalem
    All the days of your life.

6 Yes, may you see your children's children.

Peace *be* upon Israel!

Printed in the United States
151780LV00003B/15/P